RACE

Race

Kenneth Leech

CHURCH PUBLISHING
New York

First Published in Great Britain in 2005

© 2005 by Kenneth Leech
All rights reserved.

A catalog record for this book is available from the Library of Congress.

ISBN: 0-89869-495-7

Church Publishing, Incorporated.
445 Fifth Avenue
New York, New York 10016

5 4 3 2 1

This book is dedicated to the memory of my dear friend and mentor

RUTH GLASS (1912–1988),

for many years Director of the Centre for Urban Studies at University College, London, who inspired and nourished many of us to struggle, intellectually, politically and passionately, for racial justice

Contents

Preface

The questions which arise around the words 'race' and 'racism' are global, immense and complex. They need careful and sustained attention at many levels. This small study restricts its concerns to issues arising in the United Kingdom (UK), with allusions to my experience of teaching in, and visits over some thirty years to, the United States of America (US). I hope that people with a wider knowledge of 'race' internationally, or with a different knowledge based on experience elsewhere, will make the necessary connections with, and contrasts to, their own situation. A small book cannot do everything, and I have felt it wise to focus on those areas which I know best. To do so is, in my experience, often to open doors to wider networks of thought and understanding, and to throw light on places very remote from the immediate context which provoked the work. To think locally can be a way of thinking globally. Rowan Williams once remarked that we all learn our Christianity with a local accent: it is equally true to say that we all experience racism and other forms of injustice within a local context. At a certain point it is vital that connections are made with wider issues and struggles elsewhere, but if this is done too early, it is counter-productive. In order for connections to be made, there must be something to connect. So we need to begin to engage and struggle with issues where we are in order to move on. This is what I have tried to do in this book.

I want, therefore, to explore questions around the themes of 'race' and racism from a number of perspectives. I write as a white man with all the privileges accompanying that identity and position, and all the limitations in relation to the experience of racism which it brings. I write also as a Christian priest, whose life and ministry has, for much of the time, been spent in neighbourhoods which are mainly Muslim. I write as one who has encountered these realities at a practical level over some forty years of urban ministry, mostly in the East End of London, one of the most racially mixed areas in the world. I shall move from the personal to the historical, from the political to the scientific, from culture to religion, from the statistical to the experiential, and so on, I hope in a way which is not confusing. I am increasingly convinced that these matters cannot be seriously dealt with in a compartmentalized way, but only by the transgression of boundaries, by moving across artificial frontiers, and by allowing conventional assumptions to come under judgement. My aim is to raise questions, expose confusions and complexities, and contribute to the shaping of a well informed social conscience within the framework of the Christian tradition. At the same time, I hope this book will be of value to those who stand outside the Christian community. I want to 'think aloud', not to present a 'final solution' – the very phrase should set off massive warning bells – but to point to areas where we should be thinking, rethinking, acting and reflecting. This is not a field where there are simple responses, but I believe that there are guidelines and values which we ignore at our, and others', peril.

I am deeply grateful to many people who have, over many years, helped me to understand these issues better. In my early years in London at the end of the 1950s, I was greatly helped by (former Communist councillor) Solly Kaye, the late Fr Neville Palmer, SSF, the late Kathleen Wrsama, and the late Edith Ramsey. Much of my early thinking about race and racism was clarified, expanded and challenged when I chaired the student Joint Action Committee Against Racial Intolerance (JACARI) at Oxford University in 1962–3. I learnt a great deal in those years from student colleagues, many of whom have since attained academic and other distinction – Marieke Clarke, Professor Wendy James, the late Dr Sebastian Poulter, Katharine Reeves, Bishop David Russell, and Professor David Welsh. My years as Race Relations Field Officer of the Church of England's Board for Social Responsibility (1981–7) and as Director of the Runnymede Trust (1987–90) helped me to gain a wider perspective on many issues.

I am also, more generally but massively, grateful to many comrades and friends in the East End of London and elsewhere with whom I have been involved for many years in struggles against the monster of racism. In particular I am grateful to the following who have, perhaps without knowing it, helped to develop, encourage, challenge and critique my thinking on a range of issues: Kinsi

Abdulleh, the late Caroline Adams, the late Tassaduq Ahmed, Hamza Alavi, Bodrul Alom, Kaushika Amin, Julia Bard, Janet Batsleer, Chetan Bhatt, Mavis Fernandes, Professor Bill Fishman, Elaine Foster, Gerry Gable, Professor Paul Gilroy, the late Professor Ruth Glass, Paul Gordon, Savi Hensman, Shirajul Hoque, the late Archbishop Trevor Huddleston, CR, the Revd Emmett Jarrett, Dan and Denise Jones, Solly Kaye, Trisha Mata, Canon Paul Oestreicher, the Revd Eve Pitts, Dr Linda Powell, the late E. J. B. (Jim) Rose, David Rosenberg, Siraj Salekin, Anne Scheibner, A. Sivanandan and the staff of the Institute of Race Relations, Abbas Uddin, Baroness Pola Uddin, Rafique Ullah, Vron Ware, Claire Weingarten, and Julie Wood.

1 | Humanity's Most Dangerous Myth? The idea of race

Prince Charles spoke to me. He said, 'What's it like living in Bangladesh?' I said, 'Dunno, never been there.' So he said, 'What's it like living round 'ere?' And I said, ''S all right.'
(Seven-year-old Bengali boy in an East London school)

The use of race as a proxy is inhibiting scientists from doing their job of separating and identifying the real environmental and genetic causes of disease.
(Editorial in *Nature Genetics*, October 2004)

As I was writing this chapter (October 2004), a major analysis of the human genome in relation to 'race' was published in the journal *Nature Genetics*. Researchers at Howard University in Washington DC had concluded (though they were hardly the first to do so) that 'race' was a biologically meaningless concept. Every human being shares over 99.9 per cent of her or his DNA with everyone else, while the tiny variations which remain differ more within ethnic groups than between them. There was, the researchers concluded, no human population that fitted the biological definition of a race. According to this research, conventional concepts of race are dangerously misleading and should be abandoned (*Nature Genetics*, 2004, pp. S3 ff.).

This research confirmed, and gave a more solid scientific basis to, already existing findings, rather than saying something new. Although we use the word 'race' frequently, and loosely, it is in fact, in the way we use it, quite modern. Over forty years ago Ashley Montague wrote a book called *Man's Most Dangerous Myth: the fallacy of race* (Montague, 1964). The word 'race', as a way of speaking about lineage and stock (though with a firm belief in descent from a common ancestor), rather than, for example, as a way of distinguishing the human race from other animals and from plants, seems to have entered European vocabulary only in the early sixteenth century. By the nineteenth century, the idea of race as a description of some ingrained natural 'type' was well established. Although the word is widely used in many societies, and in various languages, its very use raises serious questions. Is there such a thing as 'race'? Are there such realities as 'races' within human society? Does the idea of 'race' correspond to any reality outside the minds of those who use it? If the answer to these questions is no, should we continue to use the word at all? It is necessary therefore to begin this book with a consideration of the issue of language, and to be as clear as we can about what we are discussing. This consideration must not be bypassed, for, while it is wrong to reduce all reality to language, the way we speak profoundly shapes the ideas we have and the actions we take.

It is important then that we start by paying attention to our language, and by recognizing certain truths. One of these is that the word 'race', as used in popular discourse, including sections of the media, has no clear meaning, corresponds to no known biological reality, and is of relatively recent origin. Thus racism, an idea which is rooted in the concept of race, and intellectually (though not necessarily in practice) depends upon it, is, as the currently fashionable philosopher Slavoj Zizek says, always a fantasy. So should we be discussing it at all? Yet the myth of 'race' and the reality of racism – practice rooted in, or linked to, ideas about 'race' – are sources of pain, discrimination and, at times, death to many thousands of people in the world. The issue of 'race', based on such a flimsy foundation, needs to be addressed, though the 'postmodern' obsession with 'discourse' at the expense of reality has to be resisted. 'Race' may be a fallacy and a fantasy: racism, sadly, is only too real, and damages millions of people day by day.

Up to this point I have placed 'race' in inverted commas, and I shall now cease to do so unless the immediate context requires it. I have done so because I regard it as a vague, misleading, inaccurate and confused concept. But it is tiresome to use inverted commas indefinitely, and unnecessary as long as readers get the point.

Race and racism as doctrine

The word 'racism' is often confused with 'race', but they have different meanings and different origins. 'Racism' was coined in the 1930s, though it did not enter most English dictionaries until the 1960s, and in some cases until the late 1960s. Neither racism nor racialism (an earlier usage in English) was in the *Oxford English Dictionary* in 1933. Racism appeared in *Webster's Third New International Dictionary* in 1961, though it had been missing from the 1957 edition. It was missing too from *Barnhart's Dictionary of New English since 1963*, published in 1973, while Mary Reifer's *Dictionary of New Words* (1955) included it, but only in its doctrinal sense as part of a belief system. Much of the muddled thinking around the word at present may well be related to its relative newness.

It had, however, been used much earlier, for example by the anthropologist Ruth Benedict, to describe the doctrine, rather than the practice, of racial superiority (Benedict, [1942] 1983; Caffrey, 1989). There are some other exceptions to its absence from English discourse, though significantly they relate to translated texts. (The word was familiar in French and Italian long before it became established in English.) The French philosopher Jacques Maritain used the word in his book *Scholasticism and Politics* (Centenary Press, 1940). Fr Yves Congar, who played a crucial role in shaping the thinking of the Second Vatican Council, used the word 'racism' throughout his study of *The Catholic Church and the Race Question*, published in 1953, and he defined it more in terms of practice than of doctrine (Congar, 1953). The doctrine has often been described as 'scientific racism' and has been closely linked with genetics, the eugenics movement, and notions of inborn characteristics which define some 'races' as superior, others as inferior, in intelligence, moral character, and so on. There are a range of versions of such doctrinal and quasi-doctrinal forms, from earlier crude ideas of sharp racial divisions to more recent forms of biological determinism with a strong reliance on genetic research. Biological determinism is not peculiar to race, and has been used recently in relation to gender and to homosexual orientation. The early uses of the word, as in the writings of Ruth Benedict, were associated with the doctrine of racial superiority. Benedict did, however, raise the question whether the doctrine would have been proposed at all had it not been for the fact that its basis had been laid in the violent expression of racial hatred.

prejudice + racism
distinguished

Peter Fryer has compared the relationship between racial prejudice and racism to that between superstition and dogma. Prejudice, he argues, is scrappy and oral, while racism is more systemic, and has more internal consistency (Fryer, 1984, p. 134).

Racism is clearly alive and well today, and influences today's politics. For example, people in Germany tend to see the nation as biological in contrast to the French emphasis on culture. The idea that German nationals must be born as such is still deeply rooted in German thinking. So citizenship tends to be defined as homogeneous: to be a German citizen is to have 'German blood'. 'Race' and 'nation' here are closely linked. However, this is not so in some other countries. It is estimated, for example, that over forty million residents of the US are of Irish origin, but very few identify themselves primarily as Irish. While British nationality certainly has had a racial bias, reinforced since the introduction of the concept of 'patriality' into immigration law in 1968, and even more so since the British Nationality Act of 1981, there is still a strong – though not always thoughtful – emphasis on British culture. The Parekh study on *The Future of Multi-Ethnic Britain* stressed the importance of common political culture, social cohesion and social identity rather than race or biological ancestry (Parekh *et al.*, 2000). I shall argue that the disentangling of confusions around ideas of race and culture, as well as an understanding of culture as always in process of change, is central to our task.

But it is not only misunderstanding that must cause us concern. A strong view of ethnic origin can lead to the identification of members of a nation both with genealogy and with geography, and it may be a short journey from this to what we have come to call 'ethnic cleansing': a process aimed at the purifying and clarifying of identity and membership. While 'ethnic cleansing' has been associated with serious violence, there are more genteel and bureaucratic ways of achieving it, and this also is at the heart of engagement with these issues in the future. My own view is that the quest for purity of this kind is highly dangerous and is at the root of many of our conflicts in the world today. The theme of 'purity' inevitably raises that of persons of 'mixed race'. In South America, large numbers of people are proud to call themselves *mestizos*, a term deriving from *mestizaje*, mixture. This identity is seen in some cultures as a source of pride, in others as an indicator of disgrace, in the literal sense, of impurity.

While race may remain as an idea, albeit half-digested, crude and simplistic, notions of ethnicity and culture are not static, and they change over time. Indeed living cultures are in constant flux and are invariably hybrid. In this respect, culture is similar to that equally misused word 'tradition'. The only cultures and traditions free from change, conflict and development are those that are extinct. I believe it is vital to give more attention to culture, politics and economics than to 'race' as such, while recognizing that racial ideas and racism have played, and continue to play, a crucial role in them all. I will look at the related themes of ethnicity, culture, purity and tradition later.

The study of race

Early work in the UK on 'race relations', work done mainly by social anthropologists and sociologists, tended to focus on minority communities, their characteristics, and their relationship to the 'host community'. In the US, the Chicago School of sociology, which influenced work in the UK, saw race relations as one aspect of social relations between people when they encountered racial difference. Little attention was paid to wider economic or political questions. Similarly, attention to the politics of race in the UK was very undeveloped until the 1970s. The focus was more on social aspects of the life of black communities, as in the pioneering work of Michael Banton, Sydney Collins, Kenneth Little and Sheila Patterson in the 1950s and 1960s. It was often said in this period that we knew more about the life of minorities than we did about that of the general population, and there was some truth in this claim.

These early studies tended to work on a host society/assimilationist model, and paid little if any attention to wider structural questions, or to international dimensions except insofar as they formed the colonial background to the immigration itself. The colonial background was in fact of central importance in this early work. Many of the people who pioneered the 'race relations industry' were former colonial civil servants, such as Philip Mason, and the African experience played an important part in influencing the direction of some of the British work. (Banton's work with West African seamen in East London led him to further work in West Africa itself.) But there was little attempt to connect this work with global economic trends, with the structures of world capitalism, or with international patterns of migration until urban sociologists such as Ruth Glass or geographers such as Ceri Peach entered the field. Later work by Phizacklea and Miles (1980) pushed the study of racism into the wider framework of class, housing and labour questions.

The early work on 'coloured' communities was certainly valuable, but it led to two misleading beliefs. The first was that race (and racism, a word which did not become popular until later) were only, or mainly, about minority groups, not about 'mainstream' society. Hence the absence from many of the early studies of any attention to the structural inequalities within the wider society, and the focus on 'the colour problem'. The term 'colour problem' does of course suggest that black people, or, to use the US term, 'people of colour', are the cause of racial conflicts. When I worked as a field officer for the Church of England's Board for Social Responsibility, I often addressed meetings in the white suburbs about racism, and was invariably greeted with the words 'Of course, we don't have the problem here,' which meant 'We don't have any black people.'

The second misleading belief was that minorities were located in areas so untypical of Britain as a whole that there were few, if any, implications or insights for the wider society. These ideas have remained common for many years, and they survive to this day in many places. They have helped to encourage the pseudo-objective study of 'race relations' in a way that is disconnected from the study of inequality, fragmentation and injustice in the entire social order.

The issue of 'ethnic data'

Throughout the whole area of race rhetoric and writing, we are still encountering a loose and often misleading use of terms. Take, for example, the word 'racism'. Some people seem to think that, if 'race' is an obsolete and inaccurate idea, so is 'racism' – a dangerously incorrect notion in my view. Like the word 'race', 'racism' is increasingly used vaguely, wrongly and uselessly. In some recent studies, 'racism' is used as if it were synonymous with prejudiced attitudes, prejudiced behaviour, harassment or violence. Sometimes the word is used as a term of moral condemnation. When an organization is described as racist, individuals within it feel personally insulted. Maybe they deserve to be insulted, but that is not the immediate point. At the time of writing, a member of the British National Party (BNP), an organization which would normally be described as racist if the word had any meaning at all, and was once proud of the fact, was threatening legal action against some people who had described him as 'racist' on the grounds that this would damage his personal reputation. Many now refer to 'institutional racism' although, as I shall argue later, racism is by definition institutional: this is why the word entered the mainstream vocabulary, at least in English. Some otherwise intelligent journalists seem to see the distinction between 'race' and 'racism', or 'racial' and 'racist' as one of 'fine print'. I want to suggest that there are more important issues at stake in our use of language than we often recognize.

It is therefore not surprising that confusion about language often enters into, and affects, academic research and official documents, as in the 'ethnic question' which has appeared in the British census since 1991. Much academic work, suffering from the compartmen-talization that is now common in universities, has encouraged generalizations about minority communities by studying them in isolation from wider social structures. Some writers have used terms such as 'ethnic', 'coloured', and 'race' in misleading ways, while others have become so bogged down in accumulating statistics that they have missed the underlying significance of events and move-ments behind the data.

The problems regarding census data are related to self-identifica-tion and precision in definition, but they are also linked with the political climate in the country at the time. In the US, the census, prior to 2000, saw identity very much in terms of colour, though this was in sharp conflict with the 'traditional' North American approach to identity in terms of self-definition (Hollinger, 1995). In the census classifications, the black/white divide was central to the idea of identity, which was thus reduced, in official approaches, to genetic make-up and genealogical ancestry. In the UK, on the other hand, until 1991, there was strong resistance to identifying people in the census in any way other than in terms of their name, address, occupation and place of birth.

Prior to the introduction of an 'ethnic question', the British census was careful only to identify place of birth. In principle, it was argued, place of birth was an 'objective' fact: race or ethnic origin were highly subjective and open to interpretation. Yet a focus on place of birth can also be a source of confusion as a result of popular, including media, misunderstanding and misrepresentation. Place of birth does not necessarily mean what many people think. For example, most black and Asian people in the UK were born here, while many people born in both 'Old' and 'New' Commonwealth countries were white. (I am aware of the conceptual imprecision involved in using 'black', a skin colour, alongside 'Asian', a loosely defined place of origin, but will use it for want of a simpler way of distinguishing between people of African-Caribbean origin and those from the Indian subcontinent and elsewhere.) Yet it is often assumed that most black and Asian people are immigrants, and that most immigrants are black and Asian, neither of which is true historically or currently. It has been said that 'Where are you from?' is 'the ethnic question par excellence' (Wade, 1997, p. 18), and in a sense this is true, but, in Britain in particular, it is a very loaded question. The idea that black and South Asian people are 'from' elsewhere is deeply rooted in much white British thought, but this does not make it correct. More important is the context in which the 'ethnic question' was asked. Against the background of racist immigration policies and a racially loaded British Nationality Act, the issue of why the question was being asked was bound to arise. Data gathering is never politically neutral.

These issues must lead us to ask the questions, Who are 'we'?, What is it to be American?, What is it to be British? Several books with titles like this have been written in the last few years, by, for example, Yasmin Alibhai-Brown, Nicholas Boyle, Samuel Huntington (of whom I shall say more later) and Tariq Modood. As I shall argue, these are key questions, not least for white Anglo-Saxons in the US in a period of rapid growth of the Latino population, and for white British people in a period when many British-born people are black and South Asian.

The meaning and history of race

So what does 'race' mean? The word is most frequently used to refer to a group of people with common physical characteristics, especially, though not exclusively, colour, and often associated with the claim that these characteristics are of genetic origin. This claim introduces a new dimension into what is often described as xenophobia (fear of strangers). There is little doubt that xenophobia was common in early times. Yet the ancient Greeks and Romans seem to have had no belief in white supremacy or superiority. One of the Roman Emperors, Septimius Severus, was probably black, and there is considerable evidence that ancient Greece was influenced by Egyptian and Phoenician culture. But hostility to strangers, aliens, and 'barbarians' was common in ancient times. My sense is that fear of strangers is still a major problem in contemporary Britain, and, to a lesser extent, because of rapid population movement, in the US. This fear must not be ignored, but it is not in itself a racial fear.

We need, therefore, to be careful in our approach to history in relation to race. It is generally believed that racial theories began in the eighteenth century, though some recent writers have rejected this view, dating the origins of both racial notions and racism back to ancient times. Certainly we can see many later racial atrocities anticipated in the ecclesiastical 'purity of blood' legislation in late medieval Spain, and no doubt elsewhere. In medieval Europe, for example, it is clear that in many places the nobility were seen as being of 'better blood', and the peasants as descendants of Ham, a mythology which was only much later to be reproduced in racial terms. The idea of 'black' as 'base', deeply stained in dirt, soiled and malignant, however, was common in earlier periods. The historian Raphael Samuel once said that the routine xenophobia of fifteenth-century pamphleteers 'would make a *Sun* editorial read like a UNESCO bulletin' (letter in *The Times Literary Supplement*, 19–25 January 1990, p. 63). It is important then to distinguish between xenophobia and the obsession with the idea of race. While there were myths and stereotypes relating to 'race' and ethnic origin before the seventeenth century – such as antisemitism, and hostility to indigenous people in various countries – there was still a strong sense of the equality of humankind.

The idea of race as a way of classifying human bodies seems to have been first used by the French physician François Bernier in 1684. Later, in 1735, Carolus Linnaeus used racial divisions in his classifications of human beings, and his work certainly devalued non-European people. It is here that we find the intellectual origins of modern racial thought, which Sanjek has defined as 'the framework of ranked categories, segmenting the human population, that was developed by western Europeans following their global expansion in the 1400s' (Gregory and Sanjek, 1994, p. 1).

Nobody, however, doubts that the eighteenth century was a key period for the formulation of racist ideas, not least by philosophers. Both Hume and Kant were committed to belief in the inferiority of black people. These men were not isolated figures, for the entire 'Age of Reason' was profoundly racist and ethnocentric. Rationality was seen as inseparable from the west and from 'whiteness'. Already in the eighteenth century there were thinkers who saw blacks as inhuman or even pre-Adamite (that is, belonging to a species created prior to the creation of the first man, and therefore sub-human), anticipating later 'Christian Identity' ideas. Both 'Aryan' and 'Semite' are terms which originated in the eighteenth century, though it was the rise of Darwinism that led to the formulation of the idea of race, and later of racism, into a coherent ideology. The ideas of race and racism are products of 'modernity' and are very recent ideas indeed. The origins of European racism – I use the term here in relation to doctrine or theory – are certainly connected to the Romantic movement, the historical source of 'modernity', which has rightly been seen as the womb of both nationalism and racism. It is often said that race doctrines were largely invented on French soil, but British and German influences were also present. The first theoretician of German nationalism was probably Johann-Gottlieb Fichte (1762–1814). Rousseau wrote a *Discourse on Inequality*, while ideas of racial superiority appear in Kant, Hume, Locke and others. Hume saw the difference between whites and 'negroes' as fundamental, as great in relation to mental capacity as to colour. Immanuel Kant believed that black people were incapable of pro-ducing anything of value in art and science, and that the divide between whites and 'negroes' was fundamental, not least in mental capacity. Writing of a man who was 'quite black from head to foot', Kant noted that this was 'a clear proof that what he said was stupid'. A swift reaction might be to ask, 'Who cares what Kant thought? What relevance does it have to life today?' However, Adolf Eich-mann, at his trial in Jerusalem, claimed that he had been guided by Kant's thought.

In the nineteenth century the idea of racial types, separate species with separate origins, became popular. Lamarck, writing in 1802, claimed that there were innate differences among human beings which were rooted in biology. The nineteenth century has been described as the age of 'scientific racism', to which one wing of Darwinism adapted itself. It can be argued that what we call 'social Darwinism' preceded Darwin, and the ghost of Thomas Malthus still haunts us; however, I believe that the key figure was the French writer Count Arthur de Gobineau (1816–62) whose *Essai sur l'inegal-ité des races humaines* influenced many generations of racial thinkers

(Gobineau, 1853–5; Biddiss, 1966, 1970). At the heart of this thinking was the perceived danger of the decay of civilizations through physical degeneration. Gobineau's ideas were used by many later writers including Hitler. Richard Wagner was a friend of Gobineau, while Wagner's son-in-law, Houston Stewart Chamberlain, played a key role in the popularizing of modern racist theories. Chamberlain can be seen as the key intellectual link between Kant and Hitler. There is a continuity of thought from these thinkers to later practitioners of racism.

These ideas have influenced political and intellectual history to a tremendous extent. Edward Long, justice of the Vice-Admiralty Court in Jamaica in 1774, saw Africa as 'the parent of everything that is monstrous in nature'. The work of Governor Eyre of Jamaica – who was responsible for the killing of 439 black people, the flogging of 600, and the burning of 1,000 homes after a slave rebellion – was supported by Charles Dickens, Thomas Arnold, Alfred, Lord Tennyson, John Ruskin and Anthony Trollope.

Notions of superiority, inferiority and potential decay were not linked with any one political position, but cut through most conventional divisions. For example, Hegel believed that Africans were not only prehistoric but prepolitical. Engels, writing in 1844, saw the Irish as 'little above the savages'. The British politician Winston Churchill seems to have been affected by these ideas, as was H. G. Wells. In the early years of the Labour movement, Beatrice Webb described the Chinese as 'a horrid race', 'an unclean race'. The *Daily Mail*, the first newspaper produced for mass circulation, saw itself as 'the embodiment and mouthpiece of the imperial idea . . . the articulate voice of British progress and domination'. The advance of imperialism was seen as a source of 'protection to weaker races'. British soldiers in the Second World War were told that Africans were 'as primitive as the ancient Britons'. The Duke of Windsor in the 1940s certainly upheld the 'colour bar'. In 1950 the Labour politician Hugh Dalton refused a post at the Colonial Office because he had 'a horrid vision of pullulating, poverty-stricken, diseased nigger communities, for whom one can do nothing in the short run, and who, the more one tries to help them, are querulous and ungrateful' (cited by Tony Benn in *History Today*, April 1987, p. 10).

Racist ideas spread in these years through popular culture and ridicule. For example, in 1903 the American 'cake walk', which had originated in 1898 out of fear of 'miscegenation', spread to South

London, where its fusion with the local swagger produced the 'Lambeth Walk'. Later the *Black and White Minstrel Show*, 'Nigger Minstrels', and the children's books which portrayed 'Golliwogs' and 'Little Black Sambo', helped to shape a racist background to British approaches to people of colour. For many years and in many places they were seen as people who belonged elsewhere, and often as figures of fun.

From the 1820s onwards the theme of 'degeneracy' became popular in many circles in Britain. While most of the discussion was not explicitly 'racial', and often did not mention skin colour, it is impossible to understand the rhetoric of race without taking it into consideration. The purity of the 'race' or 'stock', it was argued, was in danger through the reproductive activity of the mentally sub-normal and the 'dangerous classes', 'the mob', the inhabitants of 'outcast London'. The comparison with 'barbarians' and 'savages' was often made.

Interest in race increased in the 1860s and 1870s, the period when 'anthropometry' developed. The term 'eugenics' was coined by Sir Francis Galton (1822–1911) in 1883. Galton held that the lower classes were similar to barbarians. In the US there was a Eugenics Record Office, and one of its key figures, Harry Laughlin, author of a Model Eugenic Sterilization Law (1922), exercised considerable influence on the 1933 statute in Nazi Germany. In the US itself, a law was passed in Indiana in 1907 allowing compulsory steriliz-ation, and 20,000 people had been sterilized by the mid-1930s.

By the early twentieth century, concern with eugenics, racial purity and the prevention of degeneration had spread widely. In 1902 Rider Haggard, in *Rural England,* saw immigration into the towns as leading to the 'progressive deterioration of the race'. W. R. Inge, Dean of St Paul's Cathedral, writing in 1919, warned that in the towns the English were 'becoming darker in each generation'. Many prominent thinkers, including H. G. Wells, D. H. Lawrence and W. B. Yeats, saw eugenics as a force for positive change (Carey, 1992). Wells even called for euthanasia for the 'weak and sensual'. The popular social psychologist William MacDougall held a view of racial superiority which was rooted in biology and in the impor-tance of defending the purity of the blood. He argued that black people had never risen beyond a barbaric level of culture (Mac-Dougall, 1912, 1924). In fact, in the whole area of mental health and psychotherapeutic work, there is considerable evidence of racist assumptions, conscious or unconscious. The late Carl Jung, for example, has come under heavy fire from some writers.

In the area of politics, a simplified form of eugenics had great influence. Winston Churchill, who was British Home Secretary in 1900, called for forcible sterilization of the 'mentally degenerate', and saw 'a natural and race danger' in the rapid growth of the 'feeble-minded'. A Royal Commission on the Care and Control of the Feeble Minded was set up in 1904. In the same period, Sidney Webb warned of 'freely breeding alien immigrants', and predicted that Britain was 'gradually falling to the Irish and the Jews'. In the late 1940s Eva Hubback, a close associate of Eleanor Rathbone, was worried about the falling birth rate, and stressed the need for more white babies. She was supported in this by the socialist academic Richard Titmuss.

Those who hold the view that there is a scientific basis for 'race' tend to see human nature as biologically fixed, and believe that there is a genetic determination of intelligence and moral consciousness. The approach to 'intelligence tests' (such as measurements of IQ) is linked with this, although not all defenders of such tests hold racist views. At the same time, much so-called scientific racism is rooted in ideas of genetically determined intelligence. The Nobel Prize-winning physicist William Shockley wanted people of low IQ to be sterilized, while the Nazi regime in Germany did give an IQ test as a result of which over 320,000 people were forcibly sterilized because they gave wrong answers. In the history of eugenics, race and class are intertwined.

The story is not good, and it gets worse. There is a line of continuity between the early eugenicists and the later development of sociobiology and human ethology. Konrad Lorenz, a key figure in human ethology, compared a human body invaded by cancer to a nation infected with a population with 'inborn defects'. Each called for drastic measures. In recent years, academics such as Hans Eysenck, Richard Lynn, Chris Brand and others have stressed the importance of genetics and biology, and, whatever their own intentions, their work has been used as ammunition by racist and fascist groups. There is no doubt that racism as a quasi-scientific doctrine has exercised great power. It reached a peak in Nazi Germany, but it has not disappeared. There has in fact been a revival of 'scientific racism' in recent years. In 1974 the British politician Sir Keith Joseph warned that 'the balance of our population, our human stock, is threatened'. Some writers have referred to 'ultra-Darwinism' and biological determinism (Rose, 1998).

A key text in the history of the 'scientific' approach was an article by Arthur Jensen (1969) which provided a basis on which others have built. Much of the later thinking of the 'New Right' around race is rooted in biology and the notion of biological fixity. Biologists, sociologists, psychologists and educational theorists have drawn on these ideas. Martin Barker has argued that 'the new racism' draws heavily on sociobiology and notions of innate cultural difference (Barker, 1981). But Barker's work is now twenty-five years old, and writers such as Gilroy urge us to move 'beyond the new racism' (Gilroy, 2000, p. 32).

However, while some writers speak of a 'retreat of scientific racism' (Barkan, 1992), and even of its death, others note a revival, 'a new race science' (Kohn, 1995). One example of a journal of 'scientific racism' is *Mankind Quarterly*, founded by the Edinburgh academic Robert Gayre and taken over by Roger Pearson, founder of the Northern League, in 1978. One of its first editors was Professor Henry Garrett, an American psychologist, while contributors included Professor A. J. Gregor, who used to write for Sir Oswald Mosley, and Professor Corrado Gini, who had worked with Mussolini and spoke at the Convegno per la Cultura Fascista, described by Mussolini himself as 'a memorable event in the history of Italian fascism'. The distinguished psychologist H. J. Eysenck of the Institute of Psychiatry in London was an honorary adviser, and his book *The Inequality of Man* has been on reading lists of this and other racist groups, though Eysenck himself has always denied that there is any racist intent in his work. It is clear, however, from the literature of racist and fascist groups that they welcome what they see, perhaps wrongly, as scientific support for their views. In fact, there is no phenotypic (physically observable) or genetic difference which corresponds to cultural difference. Racial differentiation is an ideological construct. Yet these ideas continue to be regurgitated in various forms. The book *The Bell Curve* by Richard Herrnstein and Charles Murray (1994), which caused considerable controversy some years ago, drew to some extent on material from *Mankind Quarterly* (Lane, 1994). Murray sees IQ as being of key importance: brain, not nurture. A 'society of high inequalities' is inevitable unless extreme social measures are taken – raising taxes, controlling personal enterprise, and so on (Murray, 1997).

It has been suggested in a recent study that the idea of 'British-ness' itself has 'racial connotations' (Parekh *et al.*, 2000), while some historians have argued that it is an artificial construct based on Protestant religion. In fact the British are a mixture of various ethnic groups. The key period for the formation of some kind of national identity was 1066–1284, the era of the Anglo-Norman colonizing of Britain when the use of the French language became common.

In August 1964 UNESCO met in Moscow and issued a declaration that pure races do not exist within the human species. Most humans are members of more than one community, and often of more than one linguistic group. The American Anthropological Association claimed, on 8 September 1997, that the 'concept of race is a social and cultural construction with no basis in human biology'. There are no physically observable (phenotypic) or genetic differences corresponding to cultural ones. Recent work from the Human Genome Project has reinforced this view. Of course, this is denied by racist organizations who have seized on a simplified view of eugenics and sociobiology as a sort of intellectual basis for their policies. Richard Verrall, a leading figure in the National Front (NF) in Britain, expounded the biological basis for their position in the fascist journal *Spearhead* in May 1979. But these views are discredited and should not be taken seriously.

This raises the question: is race a legitimate field of study at all? Some would argue that, since the idea of race has no independent force, the study of attitudes to, and structures related to, the idea must be approached via other methods, such as Marxism, analysis of modes of production, class and so on (Miles, 1982). More recent writers have called for a 'postracial stance' (Gilroy, 2000, p. 42).

Race and other categories

While they are not the same, it is impossible to make sense of how racial categories have come to occupy a central place in political discourse without understanding some earlier debates. The social Darwinism of the late nineteenth and early twentieth centuries was often marked by a contempt for the stupid and lazy. H. G. Wells, in his book *Anticipations* (1911), exhibited such contempt, and is an important link with later discourses on race. Wells referred to blacks, yellows, and 'that alleged termite on the civilized world, the Jew'.

A word which has arisen since the 1970s is 'racialization'. It refers to the way in which populations are identified by reference to phenotypical features, understood in a biological or quasi-biological way. Again it is clear that, while race may be an unscientific and indefensible concept, much practice is based on the erection and maintenance of 'racialized boundaries' (Anthias and Yuval-Davis, 1992).

There are a number of other words and ideas which are similar to 'race' and are often confused with it. Indeed some would claim that they ought to be confused since they are alternative ways of identifying the same reality, sometimes euphemisms designed to avoid or confuse discussion.

One of these words is 'ethnicity'. Ethnicity and race are not so clearly distinguished as some may think, though they are different (Knowles, 2003). Some writers argue that all discussion of 'race' must be located within the wider category of ethnicity which provides its theoretical base. Certainly much thinking about the nation was rooted in ethnic ideas. Some would claim that there is an 'ethnic origin of nations' while others would say that nations need to transcend ethnicity if they are to avoid the more dangerous aspects of nationalism. In fact there is no necessary link between race and ethnicity. Ethnic identity is passed on mainly through language, religion and culture, not through 'race' or colour. Places such as Quebec and Barcelona are examples. Skin colour varies widely among people of the same ethnic origin. Ethnicity is generally more linked to geographical location than is race. (However, in many areas of the world, such as Colombia and Ecuador, black communities are heavily concentrated in certain areas.) Yet, historically, ethnicity and religion are often linked. Thus we speak of 'Jews' – are they a race or a religion, or both? What does 'Greek Orthodox' mean? Is it an ethnic or a religious description, or both? Are Sikhs an ethnic group, or a religion, or both? And does one have to be a Roman Catholic to be authentically Irish, or Italian, or Polish? Or the reverse? The list could be continued. The point is that these concepts are interrelated historically, but can often cause confusion and misunderstanding, and the confusion is not illusory. Large-scale migration has meant that the idea of ethnicity has, on the one hand, become more important, and, on the other hand, more unstable, fragmentary and transitional. The celebration of St Patrick's Day in the US exceeds anything that occurs in Ireland, while Irish accents are still evident in Christian communities in India, Africa, the Philippines and elsewhere. Observers in many British cities and towns have noted that, since the anti-racist movements of the 1970s and 1980s, there has been a clear shift among sections of Asian youth towards more ethnic and religious groups, sometimes with a fairly sectarian outlook.

Ethnicity is often used as if it were synonymous with race, though they are different words reflecting different ideas, while personal and national identity may not be intrinsically related to either. To identify ethnicity with race and with skin colour is to ignore vast areas of culture, language, religion, and so on. The word 'ethnicity' arose during the Second World War though the word 'ethnic' is older. It derives from the Greek *ethnos*, a people. It was used by the scientist Julian Huxley in relation to biological groups. The idea of ethnicity involves that of a group distinguished by such features as language, religion and lifestyle. It may, or may not, be associated with physical appearance, though it is significant that white people are rarely referred to as 'ethnic'. (The growth of Hispanic communities in the US may well change this. Ethnic food or dress is a euphemism for the food or dress of the 'other'. Although often used as synonymous with race, ethnicity is a different idea, although there is much evidence that the word became popular in the 1980s as a way of avoiding the specific reality of racism. The best current thought sees ethnicity not as an 'essentialist' reality, but as a process of construction and development in which there is adaptation, incorporation, amplification of earlier modes of solidarity, cultural attributes, historical memory, and so on. Writers such as Stuart Hall and Paul Gilroy are wary of the idea of ethnicity, while others stress the need to distinguish ethnic from cultural groups. It is not surprising that there is talk now of 'new ethnicities' and at least one British university has a New Ethnicities Unit. Most people in fact belong to a number of ethnic and linguistic groups and sometimes to many communities.

Again, the idea of race is often linked with that of identity. But identity cannot be reduced to genetic make-up or genealogical ancestry. Self-definition is an important issue. Most humans are hybrid. Nevertheless, writers such as Samuel Huntington, well known for his thesis of a 'clash of civilizations', have raised the question of the future of North American 'identity' in the context of significant Hispanic immigration to the US.

An idea often linked in people's minds with race and ethnic origin is that of citizenship. But citizenship does not imply a community rooted in physical descent, language and history. A civic nation rests on choice of membership. Research in Surrey in 2003 suggested that the children of immigrants are more proud to be British than are Anglo-Saxon whites. In the recent past the former British Home Secretary David Blunkett has called for an 'oath of allegiance', linked with a knowledge test, for immigrants who seek British citizenship. This can be seen as a racist idea, since white citizens have never been asked to make such an oath, and many would probably fail the test through simple ignorance, or perhaps through ideological conviction. (I have never felt able to sing 'God Save the Queen' since I do not believe in the monarchy, and find the sentiments of this song abhorrent. It would be ironic if this were to become a requirement for new citizens.)

Of course, the discussion of race has often collided with, or been fused or confused with, that of class, sometimes replacing it, often merged into it. In classical Marxist thinking, racism is seen as a post-capitalist development, and there is, I believe, some solid basis for this view. However, while Marxists have seen racism as a form of false consciousness, working against the interests of the working class, there has been a serious failure within Marxism to grasp the seriousness of racial oppression.

Much discourse in the UK, the US, and elsewhere assumes a white and Christian constituency as the norm. For example, in Norway the word used for equality is usually *likhet* which means likeness, sameness or similarity. The 'moral community' is seen as Lutheran, and, in much popular discourse, anti-Muslim. It is interesting also that in Norway the word *innvandrer* always means an immigrant. In the UK the idea of 'ethnic' rarely includes white people. This raises the question, Is white a colour? Many white people assume that to be white is not a racial identity. It is other people who are 'coloured' or 'ethnic'. Some studies, interestingly, have shown that white adolescents in the UK choose a black identity through music and cultural styles, perhaps as a result of the absence of any distinctive concept of what it is to be 'English'. Paradoxically, while white is not seen as a colour, the consequence of this view is that it is the most desirable colour. Wade, reflecting on race in Latin America, notes a process of mixedness and progressive whitening (Wade, 1997, p. 32).

Another popular word is 'pluralism'. The term 'cultural pluralism' seems to have first been used by M. H. Kallen in the US in 1924. Sometimes the use of this word is a way of talking about race without using the word. In its simple version this is no more than a recognition that there is no uniform culture. In 1971 the National Coalition for Cultural Pluralism in the US defined pluralism as the equal coexistence of diverse cultures within one nation, a form of unity combined with diversity. But it can also mean that there is a recognition that such plurality is desirable, a goal to be sought, a goal which involves equal access of all cultures to power. Pluralism is related to race but not to be identified with it, and it can be a way of evading engagement with race as a reality.

One of the most common words in current rhetoric is 'diversity'. In fact in 1990 it was found to be the most common word used in college handbooks in the US. Much thinking is still based on ideas of the 'melting pot'. In the early 1970s the group Blue Mink sang of 'turn[ing] out coffee coloured people by the score'. But inter-ethnic mixing does not necessarily lead to racial justice, and some studies have been unhelpful in this respect, such as that of Freyre in the 1950s which presented a naïvely optimistic view of race in Brazil with a glorifying of hybridity (Freyre, 1951, pp. 98–9). Things are not so simple.

Who is white? In the 1890s a light-skinned man called Plessy was prosecuted in Louisiana for travelling in a train carriage reserved for whites, although he was regarded as white in other states. Who is black? Puerto Ricans are seen as 'other' in the US but not in Puerto Rico. A study by academics at the University of Chicago in January 1991 showed that 78 per cent believed that black people were more likely to live on welfare, 62 per cent that they were lazier than whites, 56 per cent that they were prone to violence, and 53 per cent that they lacked intelligence.

Ruth Benedict, writing in 1942, was one of the earliest writers to use the word 'racism' in English. She argued that, while race can be subjected to scientific investigation, racism cannot. Racism is not scientific but is a religion and, like all religions, can only be studied historically. Michael Banton, writing in 1969, defined racism as 'the doctrine that a man's behaviour is determined by stable inherited characters deriving from separate racial stocks, having distinctive attributes, and usually considered to stand to one another in relations of superiority and inferiority' (Zubaida, 1970, p. 18).

One of the claims often made in support of allowing concessions to racial prejudice is that such prejudice is 'natural', and this is usually linked with the notion that 'you can't change human nature'. But 'human nature' is not static and immutable, and is subject to a wide range of changes related to the economic, cultural, religious and political situations and positions of a society and of individuals within it. One of the greatest challenges to anti-racist activity is that of combating and undermining all forms of 'essentialism' which portray nature and identity as fixed and unchanging.

A changing face of racial thinking?

Recently there has been a shift away from purely biological notions of racial superiority towards ideas of ethnic nationalism, sameness, and so on. This is the kind of shift which writers have in mind when they speak of a 'new racism'. This 'new racism', they suggest, is more about market forces and migrants, or about the threat to national culture. It is worth noting, however, that historically the various types of racism have often gone together. An important element in the theoretical base of 'scientific racism' has been the notion of cultural difference. The intellectual architect of apartheid, W. W. W. Eiselen, argued that if traditional cultures were destroyed, social disintegration would follow. Segregation was the only way to preserve cultural difference.

However, it is important to stress that to deny the existence of race can lead to the mistaken and illogical conclusion that we do not need to take racism seriously. I was once on a platform with a bishop, a learned man with an academic background in biology, who argued that, because race was an unscientific concept, we should not talk about it so much. I understand his point, but feel it is profoundly and disastrously mistaken. Race may be a biological fiction, but it is nonetheless a political reality insofar as policies, assumptions and actions are based on it.

At the present time there are many half-digested ideas about culture, nationality, 'Britishness', and so on. These are present in government documents, in the media, and, at a cruder level, in openly racist organizations. The proliferation of such a degree of confusion makes serious dialogue difficult, and often public utterances by political figures are a combination of cliché, partly understood academic work and populist rhetoric. It is not a healthy situation.

One concept which has come under attack from some quarters, and has been defended in others, is that of 'multiculturalism'. Most critical observers would agree that a superficial multiculturalism has done harm to the struggle against racism. This is often referred to as the 'saree, samosa and steelband' approach or, in Stanley Fish's term, 'boutique multiculturalism'. It carefully avoids areas of conflict and stresses harmony more than justice. Yet one of the ideas in multi-cultural thinking needs to be retained: the recognition that all cultures are in a state of movement, and, as they come into contact, collision or conflict with one another, further movement can occur. To avoid contact, collision and conflict is not to make progress but to delay it.

Skin colour remains of crucial importance, not least because of its visibility. But religion – for example, actual, or believed, adherence to Islam, an issue which I shall examine later – has, in Britain, added a new dimension to bigotry and violence. The stigmatizing of persons who 'look Asian' has coincided in some places with greater acceptance of blacks, African and Caribbean. They are seen as 'speaking English', and 'being Christian' (though many of the white people who take this view have a very loose connection with Christianity!). Stereotypes and mythologies change, but are perpetuated and strengthened as in the past.

People often speak of culture as if it were a static entity. But cultures are never static. They are always in transition and usually hybrid. Take, for example, the question of 'Indian' food, which is now available, and popular, in most small towns in Britain. The practice of 'going for an Indian' is a well-established part of British life. This food is in fact usually Bengali, though modified and adapted for the British clientele, and the majority of white consumers stay with a familiar number of dishes, and are confused when they encounter strikingly different ones (such as will be found in Nepalese, Goan and Keralan restaurants). 'Going for an Indian' usually refers to eating a small range of conventional dishes, usually geared to the white constituency, invented for them, often meat dishes named after Indian cities or areas which are largely vegetarian. I will return to the question of culture in Chapter 7.

What have I tried to show in this chapter? First, I have stressed the importance of taking care of our use of language, for we are operating in a field marked by shoddiness, looseness of thought and, at times, culpable irresponsibility. Christians and others have a duty to take care of their language.

Second, I have argued that it is no longer satisfactory to think of racism purely in terms of the old doctrinal or 'scientific' model, although that still exists, and has been revived in some quarters. Paul Gilroy agrees that the newer varieties of racism make no appeal to biology but view the nation as a natural unit. We need, he insists, to move 'beyond the new racism' (Gilroy, 2000, p. 32f). Others, particularly neoconservatives such as Dinesh D'Souza (1995), speak of 'the end of racism' and stress the importance of enterprise. Racism, they argue, is seen as an 'excuse for blacks to fail'. But the newer cultural racism, and the overlap between race and religion, are factors which must not be ignored, though they continue to be ignored in much 'liberal' rhetoric. The notion of 'the end of racism' is clearly simplistic and dangerously misleading. It will no doubt take its place in history along with 'the end of ideology' (Daniel Bell) and 'the end of history' (Francis Fukuyama). Like ideology and history, racism lives on.

Third, we need to see that, while the concept of 'race' is imprecise and full of uncertainties, there is no uncertainty, except among the wilfully ignorant, that racism as a practised and lived reality is alive and well. Racism as a reality degrades and does violence to many thousands of people throughout the world, and it is to racism as experienced in practice that I shall now turn.

2 | The Shape of Babylo
the reality of racism

In this country there has been a growing movement of racialism – accelerated, or tolerated, no less by well-meaning people who think that they are free from prejudice than by those who cater to prejudice. The movement, promoted in the name of 'realism', is based on the assumption that racial prejudice is immutable, and that colour problems *per se* are larger than they really are. And because such views are being spread, prejudice does indeed become more pervasive and the problems do grow.

(Ruth Glass, letter in *The Times*, 1 February 1965)

The deterioration of race relations in Britain could have been prevented. Ever since 1968 the course has been predictable (and was predicted) . . . At every step prejudice has been encouraged.

(Ruth Glass, letter in *The Times*, 4 May 1968)

The meaning of racism – from doctrine to practice

In the preceding chapter I discussed the idea of racism as a quasi-scientific doctrine. But an important shift in definition and understanding occurred at the end of the 1960s. One of the key groups in this shift was the Programme to Combat Racism of the World Council of Churches. It was at this point that the word 'racism' entered most English dictionaries. It came to be used as a way of distinguishing personal prejudice from practical discrimination embodied in structures. The term in this structural sense was popularized by writers such as Stokely Carmichael in 1967, and from this time the use of the word spread, and its focus shifted from doctrine to practice. This was not to deny that there were individuals and organizations for whom racist theories were central. But what came to be seen as crucial was stressed by two British writers in 1986: it was the belief that 'race is internal to the organization, structure and operations of the British social formation', and not an accidental or peripheral aberration (Brah and Deem, 1986, p. 72). Or, as Paul Gilroy put it at about the same time, racism is not a 'coat of paint' which can simply be wiped off to reveal tolerance and racial equality beneath the surface (Gilroy, 1987b, p. 11). Racism is about structures, about institutions, about social, economic and political processes.

The way in which racism is conceived affects the way in which it is studied, or whether it should be studied at all. Some writers have suggested that 'race' as such is not a genuine category of analysis. John Rex (1970) located race research within the framework of structural conditions such as conflict over scarce resources, class exploitation, cultural diversity, the growth of an 'underclass', and so on, while Robert Miles (1982) argued that 'race' should not be employed analytically at all. His own work focused on migrant labour, and raised questions about the usefulness of studying 'race' in isolation from wider issues. A number of writers have pointed out that racial differentiation is an ideological construction which varies from time to time and from place to place, a clear product of institutions, markets and organizations, and subject to their economic needs. These features remain major areas of debate. My own approach has been to locate 'race' within the wider framework of socio-economic and political analysis, yet continuing to stress the specific and unique character of racism within this wider framework. I do not believe that we can bypass the dimensions of 'race' and colour, or subsume them under a general notion of oppression. (This is a real danger in the new 'equalities' quango in the UK.) On the other hand, to isolate racism from social inequalities and injustices over a wider spectrum is a serious error. Equally erroneous is to see racism purely in terms of personal pathology, and this leads me to reflect on the 'therapeutic' approach to racism.

In much earlier writing, and in a good deal of 'postmodern' writing, racism has been 'psychologized'. The approach to racism by way of mental illness occurs in different forms from time to time. While Freud 'had nothing of substance to say on the subject of racism', his major anthropological study of 1913, *Totem and Taboo*, was subtitled 'Some points of agreement between the mental life of savages and neurotics'. Like many writers of his time, who had no experience of people of other cultures, he saw those whom he termed 'savages' as reflecting lower and undeveloped cultures. The psychoanalytic tradition has, with some notable exceptions, remained very narrow and naïve in its approach to racial and cultural questions (Gordon, 2001). More helpful psychological and therapeutic approaches have come from other directions, while, in the current academic climate of postmodernity, there is a danger that the use of aspects of psychoanalysis has helped to keep racism out of history and external reality, locating it rather within disturbed personal or corporate psychic histories.

More generally, we need to be careful of adopting the language of 'dangerous sickness', the description of racial prejudice used by the Declaration of Commonwealth Principles in January 1971. Well-intentioned and in many respects useful, this statement and similar ones can divert attention from the racism which is endemic within communities of 'normal' and 'well-adjusted' people (no doubt including psychotherapists). At the trial of Adolf Eichmann, a psychiatrist pronounced him totally sane. Indeed, his sanity was the problem. This is not to deny that many racially prejudiced people may have serious mental health problems, but to reduce racism to psychopathology is a serious kind of reduction with serious consequences.

One way of approaching racism psychologically has been through the idea of the 'scapegoat' as in the writing of René Girard. According to Girard, the scapegoat mechanism enables societies to survive through the management and reduction of violence. Certain groups and individuals are 'scapegoated', stigmatized, cast out from the body. Or racism may be seen in terms of excessive fear. Franz Fanon saw racism as 'the pre-logical thought of the phobic'. Other work has approached racism in terms of the degree of prejudice within a population, work which Sami Zubaida has described as 'remarkably uninformative'. Others lay emphasis on doctrine and ideological aspects. Caroline Knowles, in a recent study, warns of the danger of seeing racism in non-personal ways. Thus, she argues, the rhetoric often consists of 'empty and mechanistic assertions about the social and the political underpinning of race which are not substantiated in flesh' (Knowles, 2003, p. 27). I agree with this. Racism does not exist apart from human beings in their bodily and psychic nature.

But, important as these aspects may be, I believe that it is vital that we view racism in terms of its practical manifestations, its practice and experienced reality as a structural phenomenon. This means that no account of racism can be adequate which does not focus on such issues as housing provision, employment, and so on. We need therefore to examine racism as an experienced reality. Racism can be seen as the practical outworking of racial ideas, and this is sometimes so. However, it is often unconscious. People frequently behave in racist ways without consciously absorbing racist ideas. Practice usually precedes theory, and often replaces it. So people and organizations act in a racist way without necessarily holding racist opinions, although the link between thought and action is always complex. Phil Cohen has expressed this well:

> Racism does not become unconscious because it is institutionalized. Rather it becomes institutionalized because it operates unconsciously 'behind the backs' of its subject which it positions within these impersonal structures of power. (Cohen and Bains, 1988, p. 12)

However, having made this valuable point, Cohen seems to have moved quite swiftly toward a fashionable postmodernist posture which sees racism as so totally unconscious that all attempts to oppose it or change approaches to it are doomed to failure.

Racism is about what is the case, about practice, about the workings of organizations and the structures of society. (This is why the popular term 'institutional racism' is tautological, for racism is, by definition, institutional.) It is not simply about personal attitudes, prejudices, feelings, and so on, important as they are. It cannot be reduced to unconscious psychological activity or to the realm of fantasy. It is historically rooted, politically expressed, socially manifested, and personally experienced.

Britain as an imperial power was often perceived as being free from racism, and there were indeed many commendable aspects of imperial history. But the inability to recognize racism as a reality was linked to the 'imperial consciousness', and to the way in which events in the (former) colonies were reported. (I often encounter white people in the UK who resent the fact that people in other countries don't speak English.) British people often thought that they were free from racial oppression because, unlike the US, they had exported it to the colonies and dominions. The reporting of the activities of Mau Mau in Kenya in the 1950s is a classic example.

(Many African students in Britain found themselves nicknamed 'Mau Mau' at this time, most of them accepting the term with humour.) In fact, during these years, Mau Mau killed 32 Europeans. British persons, soldiers and others, killed around 10,000 Kenyans, while many died in concentration camps – in one case, 402 in one month. It has been claimed that conditions in these camps were as bad as those in Nazi Germany or Japan.

What of the UK itself? It was for a long time thought that the UK population was largely free from prejudice. Subsequent research has shown that the level of racial prejudice in the UK is higher than was once believed. However, even if this were not the case, the role of prejudice in relation to racism in practice is not simple. Ruth Glass's work in Notting Hill in the late 1950s led her to the belief that the size of a prejudiced group did not matter so much as its location, significance, and power within society as a whole. If the wider society was ambivalent to, or unconcerned about, racial equality, a small prejudiced minority could be more important and more harmful than a larger group within a society with more positive commitment. She concluded that 'it is because tolerance is so timid that prejudice is so infectious' (Glass, 1989, p. 191).

Philip Mason, the first Director of the Institute of Race Relations (IRR), writing in 1969, admitted that, in its early years, the Institute assumed that Britain was largely tolerant, and that racism occurred elsewhere. The sociologist Michael Banton, writing in 1953, said that 'a mild disapproval of coloured people is conventional in Britain', but believed that 'pathological' prejudice was small (Banton, 1953). For a while, this somewhat optimistic view prevailed in a number of organizations, including various governments. The major Survey of Race Relations in Britain, sponsored by the IRR, concluded that the central task was not to argue people out of prejudice, but to remind them that they were unprejudiced. Was this the 'liberal hour'? Whatever it was, subsequent reflection has shown it to be inadequate and naïve.

A British study in 1985 concluded that nine out of ten people believed that Britain was prejudiced. Fifty per cent felt that this prejudice had worsened in recent years, though only one-third admitted to being prejudiced themselves. In terms of actual personal relations, a study in 2004 in Britain concluded that 90 per cent of white people had no black friends. Of course, this does not mean that relations between black and white people may not have improved over the years: indeed there is considerable evidence that this is the case. But there is much still to be done, and it cannot all be done at the personal or interpersonal levels. However, although the terms 'institutional racism' and 'structural racism', as well as the ideas they embody, have been in use now for over forty years, there is still great resistance to them, and many writers still see them as novel ideas. When, in 1987, Linda Bellos, then leader of Lambeth Council in London, said that institutional racism existed in the Labour Party as in all institutions, the *Daily Express* described her statement as 'the unmistakable language of extremism' (9 April 1987). But what she said was demonstrably true, easily verifiable by research into attitudes and practices in local Labour constituencies.

The danger of loose, imprecise and shoddy use of language is most acute here, and one of the casualties of such use is the word 'racism' itself. Many years ago the former cabinet minister Sir Keith Joseph complained that 'the word has come to be used simply as a term of abuse to denote anyone whose feelings or views or attitudes or use of language the speaker chooses to regard as offensive to himself' (Department of Education and Science Press Release 124/86, 20 May 1986). While that statement itself is not without its problems of style and content, and is simply incorrect as an attempted statement of fact, there is no doubt that loose and thoughtless use of the word has led many to refuse to take the reality of racism seriously. The (mostly right-wing and Murdochian) tabloid press has helped to encourage the idea that 'racism' is an accusation rather than a description, and, since this section of the press does not allow much, if any, space for informed debate, the notion of racism as no more than an insult has become part of popular white consciousness. Over the last twenty years various individuals have contributed to this notion, and have therefore helped to encourage the idea that 'racism' is no more than a cliché or slogan.

Housing and other factors

Racism is manifested in structures, embodied in housing, employment, education, policing, and so on. Housing has been central to British racism since the beginnings of black immigration in the 1950s. Building societies invented 'blue zones' to exclude areas of black settlement from the market. Residents from these areas found it difficult to obtain mortgages. Black people were often housed in the worst council property. But it was many years before attention was paid to it and action taken against it. For example, there was no legislation against racial discrimination in housing until 1968, and probably no detailed study of racism and council house allocation policy until 1987. Beverley Mullings's study *The Colour of Money* (1991) broke new ground in the examination of race and local authority housing investment policies. The history is marked by lethargy and lack of real commitment as the work of the geographer Susan J. Smith has shown. The important study by Henderson and Karn of housing in Birmingham was received with hostility by the local authority. This was not surprising since the work argued that racially discriminatory practices were 'a product of the normal structure of allocations' and not 'minor aberrations' (Henderson and Karn, 1987, pp. 275, 279). Discrimination in the housing sector is of central importance.

In many parts of the world, segregation in the housing field is central to the practice of racism. In the city of Chicago, for example, the 'ghetto' districts are clearly delineated by main roads. One moves suddenly from a middle class, often white or racially mixed, area into a poor black ghetto. Research in the US, where residential segregation based on race is more marked, has made the point clearly. Thus a study from Atlanta reported:

A rising tide will not float all boats if part of the harbour is walled off from the tide. Residential segregation, which is the basis for racial separation, is the fundamental underlying structure for the inequalities which persist and continue to grow in contemporary Atlanta. (Orfield and Ashkinaze, 1991, p. 68)

After twenty-five years of regular visits to the US, I remain horrified at the persistence of racial segregation in every city I have visited. Chicago is the most extreme example. The American sociologist Saskia Sassen has expressed what has been well known for some time:

In the 1970s and 1980s our large cities became poorer and blacker and more Hispanic . . . After 1979 white city families maintained their relative standing while black families' median income declined further, and their poverty rates increased significantly. (Sassen, 1991, p. 481)

The documentation on racism in housing in the UK is enormous, though the relationship between documentation and change is often an inverse one: the more research, the less change.

Housing is, of course, related to homelessness, since homeless people are those who have fallen out, or been forced out, of the housing market. Recent work by Shelter has shown that, between 1997 and 2004, the years of the New Labour government, homelessness among ethnic minorities has increased twice as fast as in the general population – by 77 per cent compared with 34 per cent. Among African Caribbeans the figure was 89 per cent.

Employment is another major area within which racism has been, and continues to be, operative. Often the way in which the labour market operates has been attributed to 'market forces'. But discrimination in employment is not based on 'market forces': it is based on what the employer values and wishes to protect. The employment practices of the local council in Oldham were criticized by the Commission for Racial Equality (CRE) in 1993, but significant changes did not occur until after the 'riots' years later.

The question of racism within the police force has become notorious and is well documented. It has been evident in 'stop and search' procedures, in black deaths in custody, in the approach of police officers to black youth in the streets, and, more generally, in the whole ethos of the police subculture. Often it is only when well-known people are affected that action is taken. For example, police treatment of black drivers has been a source of comment for many years, but it seems only to have been taken seriously since some black people have attained senior positions in society. The Bishop of Birmingham, John Sentamu, an African and former judge, has been stopped several times while driving. Trevor Phillips, the black chair of the CRE, was stopped 34 times in ten years. My own experience of working with police over many years is that the racism within the subculture is so entrenched that it takes dramatic events to effect the slightest shift.

Within the police subculture there is often a profound lack of self-awareness and self-criticism, and an impatience and irritation with attempts to change which is often expressed in the language of cliché and sweeping generalization. Combined with this is a fierce anti-intellectualism that goes very deep. Thus Mike Bennett, former chair of the Metropolitan Police Federation, was quoted on 23 February 1999 as attacking what he called 'sociological jargon introduced by people with an agenda of their own who are determined to keep up the bogy of racism where none exists'. He went on to describe racism as 'the swear word of the 1990s'. As long as rhetoric such as this prevails, little progress will be made.

Policing brings us to prisons. The number of black prisoners in the UK increased between 1999 and 2002 by 52 per cent. By June 2000 the incarceration rate for whites was 170 per 100,000, and for blacks 1,140 per 100,000. This is nowhere near the level in the US, but, since the UK tends to follow US social policies, particularly in spheres where they have failed, it does suggest cause for concern.

Many British people seem to think that racism is a problem only of the urban areas, and certainly there has been what writers have termed an 'urbanization of injustice', a concentration of forms of injustice within cities (Merrifield and Swyngedouw, 1996). Yet the evidence that racism is clearly manifested, and may be even more serious, in rural communities is very strong. Many schoolchildren from London experience racial abuse for the first time on vacation visits to such rural areas as Devon and Somerset. I recall an incident when some children from a multi-racial primary school in Notting Hill went on a school holiday to Somerset. One child said to the head teacher, 'Miss, what's a coon?' It was the first time he had been called that, and he had no idea what it meant.

Again, there are urban areas which contain very few black people. Kamwaura Nygothi, a refugee from Kenya, wrote a tragic account in the *Guardian* (8 July 2004) of her discovery of racism in the northern town of Middlesbrough. In Kenya, she said, she had been raped, and burned with acid and cigarettes while in detention. In London she felt safe. But in Middlesbrough, for the first time, she was called 'monkey'.

> Racism is not a concept I was familiar with in Kenya, and only now that I have been moved to Middlesbrough do I properly understand what the word means . . . I escaped from Kenya because I wanted to live, but in Middlesbrough all I can think about is how much I want to die.

It is often claimed that governments do not fully understand the effects of their policies. Kamwaura, in this dreadful account of cold racial hatred, says that, in dispersing refugees to areas which have not experienced the presence of black people, the government knows exactly what it is doing.

Responses to racism

The history of political responses to racism is a sad one, and reflects little credit on the mainstream parties. On 22 November 1957 the Labour MP Eric Fletcher claimed that 'it is nobody's fault that people from overseas are content to live in conditions different from those sought by white people'. This appallingly irresponsible statement was quite typical of the evasion of responsibility for action against racism. However, no one can deny that since those days significant improvements have been made in some areas. The Civil Service has a better record than many organizations, including for many years the Church of England. (I will consider the churches' response to racism in more detail in Chapter 6.)

Within the educational field too there has been much valuable work in anti-racist education. However, one of the main dangers of the pluralist approach with its stress on multiculturalism and 'diversity' is that issues affecting black people are simply added to a white agenda which has not itself been examined. In the US, black texts were added to the 'canon' of literature studied in schools and colleges without any serious critique of the formation of the canon itself. Often, in my experience, primary schools have been way ahead of higher educational institutions, and certainly very much ahead of seminaries and theological colleges.

The theologian Reinhold Niebuhr, writing in 1932, claimed that, although there were many white people who identified with the 'Negro' cause, the 'white race' as a whole would not admit blacks to equal rights until they were forced to do so. Certainly this was also applicable to the UK. Before the 1960s racial discrimination was legal in the UK. In fact, open discrimination remained legal longer in the UK than in the US. Advertisements in house windows inviting tenants but specifying 'No Coloured, No Irish, No Dogs' were perfectly legal throughout the early years of West Indian immigration. Moreover, there was considerable resistance to the idea of making such discrimination illegal.

In the US, the role of law is more central as a way of 'solving' problems than is the case in the UK. This has been a mixed blessing, but it does mean that progress was made in some areas through use of legislation, while UK authorities relied on what David Kirp (1981) termed 'doing good by doing little'. For example, contract compliance is a way of ensuring that firms are not awarded contracts for work unless they maintain certain standards, of which racial equality in recruitment of labour is one. President Roosevelt introduced the idea of contract compliance as long ago as 1941, and two years later it was extended to all federal contractors in the US. Affirmative action, that is, action by government to reduce discrimination and disadvantage affecting minorities, was first introduced by President John F. Kennedy on 6 March 1961, and was embodied in the Civil Rights Act of 1964. President Johnson, in his Executive Order 11246 of 1965, made such action an essential part of government contracts.

In the UK Lord Listowel attempted to introduce anti-discrimination legislation in 1948, but it was resisted, and continued to be resisted. As late as 1987 the CRE, in its annual report, commented on the lack of commitment to contract compliance by the British government in 'striking contrast to its policy in Northern Ireland'. The Fair Employment Act in Northern Ireland had insisted on contract compliance, and argued against the unfairness of discrimination, in this case in relation to religion. The *Guardian* editorial of 19 December 1988 was entitled 'Where Ulster leads today', and pointed out that the legislation, which dealt only with Northern Ireland and with religious discrimination, was 'the strongest and clearest statement of aims of any anti-discrimination legislation in the United Kingdom'. Sadly the model has not been followed in Britain as a whole. What is the lesson of this? Possibly that the government takes important action on discrimination only when the situation is desperate, not simply because it is right to do so.

The 1965 Race Relations Act was the first piece of legislation in Britain to attempt to deal with discrimination, but it affected discrimination only in public places. The 1966 Local Government Act, in its famous Section 11, allowed local authorities to claim central government funding for educational needs relating to the fact that English was a second language for many immigrants. A further Act in 1968 added employment and housing to the areas of unlawful discrimination, though there is no evidence that it was effective, since the marginalized position of black people in poor housing was already established. The strongest piece of legislation was the Race Relations Act of 1976, but it came too late to affect structural racism in the housing sector, though it did allow the Department of Employment to require contractors to provide employment policies on request. Section 70 of the Act also amended Section 5A of the

Public Order Act, which had been used on occasions since the 1930s, to prohibit the incitement of racial hatred. However, cases could only proceed if they received the Attorney-General's approval. The Act was preceded by a White Paper in 1975 which stressed cumulative disadvantage and the problems of communities who were trapped in a downward spiral of deprivation. It was followed by a White Paper in 1977 which specifically avoided action against racial disadvantage. In spite of its limitations, the 1976 Act was important, not least in its emphasis on positive action to redress the disadvantage caused by earlier neglect.

It is depressing that many well-educated people in Britain, including journalists and even politicians, remain ignorant of the legislation. For example, under the Act of 1968, two government bodies were created, the Community Relations Commission and the Race Relations Board, the latter being mainly concerned with legal aspects of racism. The Race Relations Board was seen, and acted, more in terms of conciliation than of prosecution. Both were abolished under the legislation of 1976 which created one body, the Commission for Racial Equality. Yet references to, and even attacks on, the 'Race Relations Board' still appear in the press, though it has not existed for almost thirty years. (See, among many examples, Jean Rook in the *Daily Express*, 1 February 1989.) Recognition of the legislation and its importance, even the basic facts about it, has not seeped through into the consciousness of the nation as a whole.

My impression is that successive governments have attached greater importance to control of immigration – of which more in Chapter 3 – than they have to combating racism. Indeed David Lane, the first chair of the CRE, told the House of Commons on 5 June 1976 that this new body would set an example to the world, but its success would depend on strict immigration control. Significantly the CRE had no power over the operations of immigration control.

Today survey data show that more people recognize the seriousness of racism within British society. It has become clear that racist ideas are more deeply rooted than was once thought. The flip side of this is that, for many years, politicians and others have become aware that an appeal to racial prejudice can increase their popularity and credibility. When the television presenter (and now Member of the European Parliament) Robert Kilroy-Silk was removed from his TV post in January 2004 for alleged racist comments, it became clear that there was considerable public support for him in the country. However, what is crucial is the question what is the link between feelings and action? The answer is not straightforward. Prejudice may exist for years without external manifestation: but an event, or series of events, may provide the trigger that transforms feelings into action, often of a violent kind.

Many other areas of the practice of racism are well documented: for example, in employment, immigration policy, social security, the trade unions, the churches, education, and so on. Inequality in employment goes back a long way. In 1939, for example, white seamen in the UK earned £9 12s. 6d. per month, while 'lascars' (mostly Bengali seamen) earned only 35s. But inequality in employment went hand in hand with an assumption of insignificance. During the Second World War, at least 6,800 lascars were killed at sea, but the monument on Tower Hill to 26,833 seamen contains very few Asian names.

However, there is what appears to be a deliberate fragmentation and compartmentalization within official reports on a range of subjects so that only a small part of the issue is examined. The authors then, rightly, insist that to discuss wider issues was 'not in their brief'. This phenomenon has been evident in recent inquiries commissioned by the Blair government, leading, in one well-publicized case, to a refusal of cooperation with the inquiry by a major party. In the field of race relations, the Scarman Inquiry of 1981 into the 'Brixton disorders' in South London is a good example ([Scarman], 1981). Scarman admitted that social conditions created a predisposition to violence. But of its 124 pages, 91 were about the police, only 22 about social conditions, seven about the law and one about the media. In relation to long-term causes, Scarman said that this was 'a field which it is for others, not me, to cultivate' (6.4). The Scarman Report was interesting also in that it was based on the idea of an 'integrated' society within which problems could be dealt with through cooperation, reforms and work toward a 'fair deal' for all. The idea that exploitation, and therefore conflict, might be basic to that society did not cross his mind. And why should it have crossed his mind? Consciousness of racism calls for a dramatic shift in perception, and this is difficult within a class system.

This is not to say that no others have helped to cultivate the field, though it remains true to say that we know more about the social conditions of some ethnic minority populations than we do about those of the population as a whole. More generally, the compartmentalizing of the study of 'race relations' or 'ethnic relations' within academic units has not helped people to grasp the wider picture. This concern with 'fragments' is often seen as a feature of postmodernism, but it was very much in place before the word was known.

What is much more difficult to document is the more subtle manifestation of racism in language, assumptions, innuendo, and the like. Certainly there has been a change in the kind of language which is tolerable, though this too is variable. In 1989 the Recorder of London's use of the term 'nig nog' led even the *Sun* to call for his removal. However, the writings of the *Daily Star* columnist Ray Mills over a long period led the Press Council to refer, in 1987, to his 'outrageously racist, crude, offensive and inflammatory remarks'. Crude material of the Mills type has probably diminished in the 'mainstream' press, though much of the really inflammatory material has been transferred to the internet. Yet racist jokes are still common at right-wing gatherings.

Much media writing sees race as a 'problem'. (As we have seen, before the word 'racism' was in widespread use in the UK, the term used was often 'the colour problem'.) Much of this rhetoric appeared in the UK media over the years. A well-known judge, Lord Denning, made a number of appalling and simplistic utterances about black people. One of the most popular British daily newspapers, the *Daily Telegraph*, is full of highly prejudiced material on a more or less daily basis. George Gale, a regular columnist for the *Daily Express*, wrote an article on 3 March 1989 in which he argued that 'we' [presumably white British people] should 'do nothing which shores up their [presumably immigrants'] alien culture'. Examples of this kind of writing run into many thousands. A depressing example of the populist clichés occurred in 1988 in words attributed to one Christine Smith, a Conservative councillor in Waltham Forest. Ms Smith spoke of 'anti-racist insanity'. 'We are sacrificing our country on the altar of race relations. England, a sacrificial lamb, has turned into halal meat . . . Ethnic languages, ethnic cultures, ethnic religions are taught in our schools, almost to the exclusion of British culture, English language, and the Christian way of life' (cited in *City Limits*, 13 October 1988). A teacher might have been tempted to use this in an examination paper followed by the question 'What is wrong with this collection of statements?' Sadly, statements of this kind are still reproduced on a daily basis.

More serious perhaps (though this is questionable) than the explicit racist rhetoric of the 'gutter press' is the misrepresentation of studies and reports by various sections of the media, which then acquires authoritative status. Thus the Parekh Report of 2000 made the fairly obvious point that the concept of 'Britishness' had 'racial connotations' (Parekh *et al.*, 2000). In many newspaper reports, 'racial' quickly became 'racist', and some papers claimed that the report had urged us to stop using the word 'British' altogether. One highly respected and intelligent journalist claimed that the distinction between the words 'racial' and 'racist' was one of small print.

A major problem in this whole area is that of denial. As with alcoholism, where many individuals spend years denying that they are addicted, so, in relation to racism, many public figures spend years denying the existence of racism until political and other changes make this posture impossible. 'There is no racism in the Conservative Party', Mrs Thatcher assured us in 1984. 'I will not have the Labour Party called racist,' cried former leader Neil Kinnock in 1987 – words uttered, ironically, on May Day, that feast of universal equality. The journalist Paul Johnson, a 'recovering socialist', once wrote in response to the claim that Britain was racist: 'Sensible people will yawn, sink deeper into their summer deckchairs, and mutter "Baloney! Britain is not a racist country and never has been"' (*Daily Mail*, 8 July 1991).

Sadly this kind of language is not peculiar to the right-wing tabloid newspapers. In Britain today, it is common to hear politicians deny that mistrust of foreigners is a key element of English history. In fact, there is abundant evidence of racism in the history of the mainstream parties. Within the Conservative and Labour parties, it has sometimes assumed quite open and crude forms. More often it has been disguised and obscured, in the former by the rhetoric of paternalism, in the latter by vague notions of 'the brotherhood of man'. The Scarman Report rejected the idea of 'institutional racism' entirely on the grounds that, if it existed, it must have functioned 'knowingly', though it recognized that the possibility that racism operated 'unwittingly' deserved 'serious consideration'.

Sometimes denial seems to be linked to straightforward ignorance. Thus the Conservative MP Nicholas Budgen, writing in the *Daily Mail* on 13 March 1996, claimed that while there had been 'black riots' in Brixton, Bristol and Wolverhampton, there had been 'no white rioting'. This is, of course, nonsense, as even a reading of the newspapers would have shown. Some might say that MPs do not have time to read the newspapers. Yet the plea of ignorance is not a good excuse for racist rhetoric. Many of the people who utter statements of this kind are quite well educated, have better access to 'information' (though not necessarily to knowledge or wisdom) than many of us, even have researchers who can check the facts for them if they are genuinely ignorant. My sense is that they are not simply stupid or ignorant, but prejudiced, imprisoned within the stereotypes and norms of their class and cultural position. Education in its conventional sense will not help them. What is needed is not 'education' in the conventional sense but a radical change of perspective.

It seems clear too that politicians, black and white, once they attain power, have a tendency to exaggerate the degree of progress which has been achieved. Thus the Labour MP Keith Vaz, himself a black person, recently claimed that 'since 1997 Britain has had a pretty good record on race issues' (*Guardian*, 21 May 2004). Such statements are both misleading and contribute to a state of complacency. Of course, in comparison with some parts of the world, this is correct, yet, as a bald statement of what has been achieved in relation to what needs to be achieved, it is dangerous nonsense. Recognition of progress is right: failure to admit defects is irresponsible. In this, sadly, many co-opted blacks follow the white mainstream line.

Part of the reason for this line is, I think, that white people are the only people in the world who have never, as a group, experienced systemic racism. This, of course, is not to say that individual white people have not experienced racial prejudice or discrimination. Clearly there is much prejudice, and often racially based behaviour, against whites, but, because the power structures of the world are mostly in white hands, the experience of racism as a structural reality is unknown to most white people. As a result it takes a great deal of emotional and intellectual effort to treat it seriously.

In the US it seems clear that the corporate sector has embraced affirmative action mainly by choice, and minorities now form a large percentage of middle to upper parts of firms. In the fifty 'best companies for minorities', these groups currently represent around 24 per cent of managers and senior officials. Affirmative action has achieved a great deal, though it has its critics, including black academics such as Thomas Sowell, and there is much current debate in the US about its limitations and allegedly adverse effects on the morale and sense of self-respect of minorities. It is claimed that those who benefit are mostly black professionals who already have 'one foot on the ladder'. There is some truth in this, and there is little doubt that what is termed 'the underclass' has not benefited from it. Much of the attack in fact comes from black professionals who have 'done well'. In spite of such opposition, numerous studies have shown its value. Indeed some of its critics might not have been in their present positions without it. After all, racism was official policy in what is now the US for 335 years, from 1619 to 1954.

However, while positive discrimination in the North American sense – that is deliberate discrimination in favour of minorities to reverse the effects of earlier discrimination against them – is illegal in Britain, the 1976 legislation does allow for 'positive action' (Sections 35–38), a similar term to affirmative action. It was this provision which made it possible for Lambeth Council in South London to establish equality targets in housing after 1979, and to house more black families (Ouseley *et al.*, 1981). More recently, a scheme in Tower Hamlets to increase the numbers of Bengali and Somali social workers has been very successful. Since the launch of the Positive Action scheme there in 1998, 70 per cent of the 106 recruits have been Bengali, and 16 per cent Somali. As a result, by 2004, 14 per cent of the council's 405 professional social workers were Bengali.

Throughout the second half of the twentieth century, there was, in my view, a refusal to face the reality of racism head on. The residual imperialism which still infected the leadership, and other sections, of the British political machine made it particularly difficult to respond to the issue, or to know what they were responding to. What was the object of the exercise? What were we hoping to achieve? Roy Jenkins, Home Secretary in 1966, and one of the first to take 'race relations' seriously, thought in terms of 'integration'. He saw this 'not as a flattening process of assimilation', but rather as one which involved equal opportunities, cultural diversity, and mutual tolerance (Deakin, 1970, p. 23).

As I look back on those years, I wonder whether a major part of the problem was a lack of confidence in the whole concept of equality. Racial equality makes no sense unless there is an underlying commitment to human equality. Yet it is easy to slide into a pseudo-commitment to human equality which denies the specific character of race. David Kirp argued that much British policy in those years was determined by 'racial inexplicitness'. 'Race may be a predicate for positive policy as long . . . as no one takes official notice of the fact' (Kirp, 1981, p. 2). The 1968 Urban Programme focused on special needs, and certainly helped minority communities, but the more explicit language of 'racial disadvantage' was becoming popular in this period. Certainly black people were disadvantaged, but the use of 'disadvantage' instead of 'discrimination' did, unintentionally or not, reinforce the idea that racism was a kind of cultural defect or pathological condition that could be helped by education and other forms of improvement of the disadvantaged, rather than a systemic condition requiring action against the discriminators.

Also at this time the forces of opposition to anti-racist legislation were mounting. Enoch Powell's speech of 20 April – which became known as the 'rivers of blood speech' – set the already half-hearted project back, and, in the words of *The Times* on 11 July 1968, 'did lasting damage to race relations in Britain'. I will say more about the role of this politician in Chapter 3. Powell was in many respects a lonely and tragic figure: his enduring success in making race relations worse was due in part to his own charisma, but more to the lack of strength and courage of the forces working for racial justice. Where tolerance is timid, prejudice is infectious. Thus, in the absence of positive forces on the other side, this person was able to appeal to the gut feelings of many ordinary white people who felt ignored, neglected and forgotten. It could have been different, and we are still dealing with the legacy of this dreadful phase.

From its beginnings anti-discrimination legislation and action was ridiculed in the 'gutter press'. This hostility reached its peak in the 1980s. Educational policies relating to race in the London Borough of Brent, while praised by the Inspectors of Schools, were ridiculed in many newspapers who referred to Brent's 'race spies'. The collection of ethnic data was also ridiculed and opposed, though this was a late development in most British institutions (although the Employment Exchange in Settles Street, East London, kept such records in the 1940s).

However, it needs to be emphasized that race relations legislation has never been as effectively or as enthusiastically pursued as that relating to immigration. As we shall see, the two are intertwined in a way which cannot be seen as wholesome. Discrimination is often hard to prove, and the burden of proof has fallen on the applicant. The procedures have been very cumbersome, and there has been little precise checking of the legislation. The 1976 Act was not effective in the field of employment where more positive action was needed (McCrudden *et al.*, 1991). In immigration law – which is not subject to the race relations legislation! – the opposite is the case. (Racism at the doors of Britain is acceptable, indeed is seen as a way to reduce it within Britain.) The concept of 'patriality', embodied in 1968 legislation, which was condemned by the European Commission on Human Rights, was abandoned in 1981 in favour of a vague notion of 'a close connection' with Britain. In this period there was a definite racial loading of ideas of citizenship and nationality.

It was during the Thatcher years that the Falkland Islands war took place. It may have revived the 'spirit of Britain'. It also led to a modification of the British Nationality Act, enabling the Falkland Islanders to have right of abode in the UK. One peer said in the House of Lords that, while he could not define a British citizen, he knew one when he saw one. Those islanders are, of course, white. I have often wondered if, had they been black, the war would even have been fought. But they were, as we were told at the time, 'our own people', a crucial and revealing phrase. It was during these years also that the obsession with illegal immigrants, linked in Mrs Thatcher's mind and speeches with terrorism and drugs, became a more central political concern. Indeed the virtual electoral collapse of the National Front at the General Election of 1979 which brought Mrs Thatcher to power was connected with the belief that the Conservatives would now achieve what the National Front could only talk about – the end of immigration. This obsession with an 'alien wedge' stood in sharp contrast to the lack of commitment, moral and financial, to combating discrimination within the UK itself. Both the Commission for Racial Equality and the UK Immigrants Advisory Service regularly complained of inadequate support.

Tragically, though predictably, as the Liberal politician David Steel said in 1978, 'the racialist extremism of the sixties' had 'become the respectable orthodoxy of the seventies'. I will say more about this later in relation to attitudes to immigrants. But there is a general point which is really important: the fact that the articulation, and practical manifestation, of prejudice and hatred inevitably leads to more of the same. That dedicated campaigner for racial justice, the late E. J. B. (Jim) Rose, commented in the late 1980s that 'race issues have made cowards of our politicians' (*The Times*, 31 January 1989). Racism came to be taken for granted, so built into our structures and consciousness that no mainstream politician seemed willing or able to break the terrible cycle.

At the time of writing there is debate in the British press about a possible merger of the CRE with other bodies concerned with discrimination in relation to women, disability, and so on. The CRE was itself the result of a merger, and many would argue – as Margaret Legum did at the time – that it would have similar effects to those resulting from the 'streamlining' of social services after the Seebohm Report. I certainly fear that widening the scope of the concern with discrimination, without a rigorous commitment to specifics, will achieve little about anything, while the class of bureaucrats shuffling thicker wads of papers will continue to flourish.

The situation today

In the years after 1958 research on the new immigrants was dominated by the newly formed Institute of Race Relations, which had grown out of the Royal Institute of International Affairs and became an independent body in 1958. Under its director Philip Mason, the Institute – based in Jermyn Street, in one of the most affluent districts of the West End, where black faces were rarely seen – was a crucial source of information for journalists and students of this expanding research area. But it also located the study of race firmly within a cultural climate which supported the established order. Studies focused on black minorities, with little or no attempt to relate them to wider aspects of class and social stratification, still less to the structures of the British state as a whole. The Institute was forbidden by its charter from expressing any 'opinion': it studied racism from many miles above the battle, providing 'neutral' and 'objective' information; what were called 'facts', rather than ideology or opinion.

One approach to racism has been the movement known as Racism Awareness Training. Originating from the work of Judy Katz in the US, this approach has been accused of seeing racism as 'a temporarily disfiguring individual disease' (Amrit Wilson, 'Therapy for racism', *New Statesman*, 13 July 1984). There have been many psychological accounts of the origins of racial prejudice and bigotry, focusing on such areas as the need to exclude 'the other', hatred of strangers, the threat to sexual purity, the urge to aggression, and so on. I have no wish to denigrate these approaches, or to deny the importance of the deep emotional roots of prejudice. But there is a danger that the actual reality of tackling racism as it occurs is side-stepped and reduced to the realm of personal therapy. I have no doubt that many prejudiced individuals could benefit from therapy, if they could afford it: and this raises the question of the relationship between prejudice and deprivation. But I cannot see why black people and others on the receiving end of such prejudice should be expected to wait until these people have been persuaded to undergo such therapy, and until the process has had some effect. Many thousands will have died in the meantime. And, crucially, this ignores the fact that much, perhaps most, racism is perpetrated by 'normal' and 'well-adjusted' people. The realization of this is central to our understanding. Not only is racism not synonymous with personal prejudice: it is more normal than it is abnormal in our society. The psychiatrist who declared Adolf Eichmann perfectly sane was making a point worth remembering. No doubt some of the leaders of racist and fascist movements have been, and are, seriously mentally deranged and at times psychotic. But to ignore the appeal of racism to ordinary, 'normal' people is a disastrous error.

What is missing in much of this sort of approach is any sense that racism is historically rooted. Those who emphasize personal prejudice, immaturity, lack of 'consciousness' and so on tend to take racism out of history, and their role is thus limited to an idealist and ahistorical realm. Phil Cohen has put the point well:

> It is certainly the case that there have been plenty of racist ideologues who have drawn on the language and philosophy of irrationalism, albeit in a highly calculating way: but it would clearly be absurd to conclude from this that all racists are suffering from a special kind of thought disorder or emotional disturbance! The project of constructing some mass psychology of racism has always foundered on the fact that, whatever instance of psychopathology is identified with extreme racist beliefs, it can also be found distributed just as widely amongst other populations. There are plenty of 'rigid authoritarian personality types' to be found in the anti-racist movement, for example, and it may well be that some of them are splitting off or repressing the 'bad' parts of the Self,

associated with excretory functions and projecting it onto The Other in the form of white racists! However, to regard racist or anti-racist attitudes as simply a rationalization of conflicts located elsewhere in the psyche, rather than in society, is in itself a rather interesting example of displacement. Therapeutic models of intervention based on such ideas are either impracticable – you cannot lay a whole society out on the couch – or else treat the problem as having to do with a deviant minority, rather than being the social norm that it is. (Cohen and Bains, 1988, pp. 88–9)

It is important to say that much of the current language about 'inclusion' and 'diversity' evades and obscures the reality of racism. It is also often a form of mystification. 'Inclusion' can often mean that groups and individuals who fit certain criteria are included, or simply that they are physically present though they play no significant role. 'Diversity' can be seen as an end in itself, while inequality and oppression remain unchallenged. Hazel Carby has pointed out that the politics behind the rhetoric of identity and difference is little concerned with the complexity of racialized structures of domination. It speaks about oppression and resistance, but not about systems of exploitation and certainly not about revolution (Carby, 1999, p. 99). Over thirty years ago the sociologist A. H. Halsey observed that much of the writing on race focused on immigrants but neglected the fundamental issue of equality (Halsey, 1970). His words abide.

It is worth saying something finally about the idea of a 'race relations industry'. This term originated with left-wing, often black, critics of central government policy. Two of the earliest uses of the idea occurred in an article by John Gretton, entitled 'The race industry', in *New Society* on 11 March 1971, and in one by John Downing, a former Anglican priest in East London, entitled 'Britain's new industry: harmony without justice', published in the journal *Race Today* in October 1972. Sivanandan, director of the Institute of Race Relations, used the term 'race industry' in 1974, as did his colleague Colin Prescod in *Race and Class* (Autumn 1979). The term appeared also in a report by Counter-Information Services in 1976. It was much later, in the Thatcher period, that the term was taken over, and used increasingly as a cliché, by right-wing populist newspapers and journalists. It is difficult to be sure whether they were ignorant of its origins, and had simply picked it up from the dominant vocabulary, or whether there was a more subtle political strategy of using the language of 'the enemy' for their own very different ends. My sense is that the former is more likely to be correct.

Thus an editorial in the *Daily Mail*, a very right-wing newspaper indeed, said on 11 March 1982: 'We have a race relations industry to speak for the coloured communities. But who will speak for these frightened and frail white prisoners of Britain's new urban ghettoes?' Six years later the journalist Melanie Phillips called on the government to 'shut down the race industry' (*Sunday Times*, 20 December 1998).

The motives of such statements – which have now become part of the daily vocabulary of the right – may well be questioned, and no doubt many of those who make such statements may have little concern for racial justice, or for justice for anyone. Yet it would be foolish to ignore this kind of utterance simply because right-wing media millionaires have finally taken it over. There will be no racial justice unless there is justice for all people. While there are many reasons to be concerned at the extent of racism in Britain, we are not without grounds for hope. History suggests that, at moments of social, economic and political crisis, black and white people often come together in solidarity against the oppressive power structure. This was true in the Alabama coalfields of the early twentieth century (Kelly, 2001), and it was certainly true in London at various points in the 1960s and beyond. The position today, however, is very complicated. On the one hand, there is undoubtedly more recognition of the need to combat racism than was the case a few decades ago. On the other, there is too much moral and symbolic anti-racism, imposed from above in thoughtless and 'trickle down' ways. Only a committed, renewed and passionate grass roots movement against racism can overcome the clear tendencies towards more and more bureaucracy, more and more rhetoric, less and less action.

3 | 'Just Deportees': issues about immigration

It was their labour that was wanted, not their presence.
(A. Sivanandan (1981–2))

All we do is implement the rules. My members merely carry out what we are told to.
(Head of the British Immigration Service Union, cited in the *Independent*, 15 October 1986)

'I don't understand my own country any more,' I said to her. 'In the history books they tell us the English race has spread itself all over the darn world: gone and settled everywhere, and that's one of the great splendid English things. No one invited us and we didn't ask anyone's permission, I suppose. Yet when a few hundred thousand come and settle here, among our fifty millions, we just can't take it.'
(Colin MacInnes, *Absolute Beginners*, MacGibbon and Kee, 1959, p. 189)

The argument boils down to this: colour discrimination is proper in some respects but improper in others. It is necessary at the doors of Britain so as to reduce it within Britain.
(Ruth Glass, letter in *The Times*, 5 August 1967)

The discussion of race in the UK, and to a certain extent in Europe, has been marked for many years, and in some cases centuries, by a highly charged level of polemic about, and against, 'immigrants'. In the twentieth and twenty-first centuries, most, though not all, of this polemic has been about, and against, black people. It has recently been intensified by the idea that Britain is a 'soft touch' for refugees and asylum seekers, who, it is widely believed, are 'flooding' into the country and receiving privileges not available to the native-born population. Water has become mixed with meat extract to produce what Tony Blair described as 'the gravy train of legal aid' – though it seems to be a train which is only attacked when immigrants are involved. As recently as 19 February 2004, the *Independent* was referring to 'fears that Britain would be flooded by migrants'. (Though, running alongside this rhetoric, has been another in which there has been talk of 'exploding cities' and 'the urban time bomb', often linked with the presence of black people. It is not clear how so much water can stoke so many fires.) At the Conservative Party conference in October 2004 the shadow Home Secretary warned that immigration 'endangers the values that we in Britain rightly treasure'. It seems that, in the desperate rush for votes, the major parties are adopting the clothes and the rhetoric of the racist and fascist groups which have, until recently, been on the fringe of British politics. This was clear in the rhetoric around immigration in the run-up to the British General Election in May 2005. But this is not new, as I shall demonstrate.

In fact much of the rhetoric is unbalanced and often plainly wrong. Most asylum seekers do not come to the UK or to Europe at all, while most migrants are not asylum seekers. Between 1995 and 1999, 80 per cent of migrants to the UK were from 'developed' countries, most of them white. Most people who come to the UK do so to work or to study. Moreover, the idea that the UK is a 'soft touch' for immigrants is almost the opposite of the reality. In 2000, although the UK received 78,000 official asylum requests, only 10,000 were given refugee status; 75 per cent of the applications were refused. Refugees in the UK in 2003 formed less than 0.2 per cent of the population. Between 1990 and 1996, 1.5 million applied to Germany, compared with 224,000 to the UK. Between 1999 and 2001 acceptance of asylum seekers by the UK was below the European Union (EU) average. The UK came 12th in the EU for admission of asylum seekers, and 11th for refugee admissions. In 1993, for example, the UK received 1.8 million foreign persons, compared with 5.2 million who went to Germany and 3.6 million to France.

But the story involves issues wider than Europe, to which less than 5 per cent of asylum seekers come in any case. The vast majority go to 'developing countries', usually neighbouring ones, while, in the 'developed' world, North America has replaced the UK as a zone of preference. However, contrary to popular belief, of the 12 million or so refugees in the world, 72 per cent have been given asylum by developing countries. Under 2 per cent of the world's refugees were living in the UK in 2002, though a MORI poll in May of that year suggested that most British people believed that the figure was around 23 per cent. In 2003 the UK, the fourth richest country in the world, came 34th in its support of refugees. Fears that the eastward expansion of the EU after 2004 would lead to massive increases in immigration to the UK seem not to be justified by research.

It seems correct to say, however, that a very large section of the white population have accepted uncritically the racism and hysteria of the popular press. In a poll of September 1993 for the *Sunday Express*, 36 per cent of whites said that they would support the 'forcible repatriation' of immigrants, while ten years later a MORI poll reported that 34 per cent of those interviewed believed that immigration was the biggest problem facing Britain. During the debates around 'citizenship tests' from 2002 onwards, Angela Eagle MP claimed that a fee of £35–40 for citizenship was reasonable, and compared it to a marriage ceremony. The idea was greeted with enthusiasm by the far right US politician Pat Buchanan in the pro-motion of his book, whose title (reminiscent of Oswald Spengler) was *The Death of the West: How Mass Immigration, Depopulation and a Dying Faith are Killing our Culture* (2002).

A more recent study has suggested that hostility to immigrants has grown since New Labour came to power in 1997. According to the 21st British Social Attitudes Survey, published in December 2004, not only did government ministers, particularly David Blunkett, at that time – though not for much longer – the Home Secretary, appear more hostile to immigrants, but so did the general public. Inter-viewing 3,000 people in 1995 and 2003, the survey concluded that the proportion favouring stronger controls had risen from 78 to 82 per cent. Among graduates, the proportion favouring reduction of numbers had risen from one-third to 56 per cent, while among those with no qualifications, the figure had slightly fallen from 82 to 81 per cent. Among both Labour and Conservative voters, the numbers wanting tighter controls had increased, from 58 to 71, and from 71 to 84 per cent respectively (*Guardian*, 7 December 2004).

It is worth remembering, however, that, while we are familiar with the rhetoric about immigration, it is not all that long ago that public figures were encouraging emigration *from* Britain. Thomas Carlyle, in the nineteenth century, urged state-aided emigration and the distribution of white people throughout the world. Cecil Rhodes sent British workers to South Africa as a way of curbing social unrest in Britain! In the 1920s Conservative MPs supported the exporting of people to South Africa and Rhodesia as a way of reducing over-population in Britain. Throughout much of the time since the 1960s when anti-immigrant agitation has been strong, emigration from Britain exceeded immigration to it.

'Race' and immigration are often linked together in confusing ways, though there are genuinely important connections. The British debate on race, unlike that in the US until recently, is inextricably bound up with the arrival of immigrants, originally from the Caribbean and later from India and Pakistan. However, certain clarifications and distinctions are important. Much of the British press, and many political figures, have often written or spoken as if most immigrants were black, and as if most black people were immigrants. In fact, for many years the majority of immigrants to Britain have been white, while over half of the black population in Britain was born here. At the time of agitation for controls in the late 1950s and early 1960s, black Commonwealth migrants were heavily outnumbered by Irish and Europeans.

Although the debate on immigration has focused on numbers, the colour and character of the immigrants has always been a factor, usually the major one. Since the eugenics campaigns of the late nineteenth century, there was concern that immigrants to Britain should be 'of the right type'. The Royal Commission on Population in 1949 stressed the need to guarantee that immigrants were 'of good human stock', and were 'not prevented by their religion or race from inter-marrying'. More recently, as one might expect of a neoliberal economy in which the market rules, the focus has been less on biology than on affluence and economic viability. It is not surprising that migrants from 'developed' countries (mostly white) formed almost 80 per cent of the inflow to the UK between 1995 and 1999. Today the largest group of global migrants consists of executives of transnational companies. So, while many migrants move to another country as a result of poverty, there are other factors – such as military and business links, foreign investment which is aimed at production for export, and so on – which affect the geography of migration.

Again, most white British people do not seem to realize that immigration to Britain has been an integral part of its history for centuries. The Labour politician Robin Cook put the point well in 2003:

London was first established as the capital of a Celtic country by Italians who were in turn driven out by Saxons. Our great cathedrals were built by Norman bishops, and the religion practised in them was settled by a Dutch prince. (*Independent*, 19 December 2003)

Black people too have been residents of the country for a very long time, probably going back to the Roman invasion. Certainly there were many British-born black residents around 1500, enough to incur the wrath, some years later, of Queen Elizabeth I who sought the removal of 'blackamoors' from the kingdom. But until the 1950s the black communities were small and relatively concentrated, and research in the mid-1950s suggested that half of the British population had never met a black person.

Today the world situation has changed dramatically in terms of human mobility (although it is worth remembering that in the US, viewed as one of the most mobile populations in the world, a very small percentage of people possess passports). Global political and economic conditions in recent years have increased the likelihood that large-scale migrations, many of them including poor as well as affluent people, will occur, and that the areas of mass emigration will be those where extreme hunger, poverty, war, oppression and persecution are prevalent. There are around 120 million migrant workers and refugees in the world, and some 30 million displaced persons. Many migrant workers send two-thirds of their income to their families at home, and many areas are entirely sustained oy these remittances. According to the International Labour Organization, there is an annual flow in remittances of at least $100 billion which recently was double the annual global aid budget.

Immigration has, of course, been an important element in the growth of many countries for a long time. The US, Australia and Canada are obvious examples. Since the early settlements, immigration to the US has been over 55 million, the largest movement of people in recorded history. In the nineteenth century, as a result of poverty, a large number of people – about the size of the population of Norway – migrated to the US. The vast majority of the population of the US today are immigrants or descendants of immigrants. The US is the only 'First World' country to share a 2,000 mile border with a 'Third World' country, Mexico, and this has recently become a key factor in American politics. This is not to deny that there are other global forces than poverty which contribute to migration: military and business links, and issues related to foreign investment policies are equally significant.

British cities since the Industrial Revolution have absorbed migrants from within Britain as well as those from overseas. In Victorian Britain, more people died in cities than were born in them, and cities were constantly being renewed by migrants, though these came mostly from other parts of the country. Writers constantly claim that the history of London is the history of its immigrants, but this is only partly true. Internal migration was more significant. Between 1851 and 1911, for example, many of England's rural counties lost population to the cities. Both internal migration and immigration from outside Britain played important roles in the life of East London, and this was true of London as a whole. Indeed London, like New York, was largely built up in the nineteenth century by what we today call economic migrants. The need for labour was crucial, and remains so to this day. Between 1956 and 1961, 4,500 Barbadians were recruited by London Transport and by various hotels and restaurants. Other West Indians were recruited to help the National Health Service to survive. But, as Sivanandan wrote in 1982, 'it was their labour that was wanted, not their presence' (Sivanandan, 1981–2). His words remain true. In the US the conservative Cato Institute has described immigrants as 'the lubricant to our economy'.

Hostility to refugees and 'economic migrants' is not new either. Media agitation in 1902 prefigured that of later years, almost in the same language. Thus the *East London Observer* on 18 January 1902 reminded its readers: 'This is England. It is not the backyard of Europe. It is not the dustbin of Austria and Russia.' It ended its polemic with the slogan 'No rubbish to be shot here'. It is worth comparing this with an editorial in the *Daily Star* on 21 November 1995, which, after insisting that Britain cannot have an open door policy, ended with the suggestion that posters should be put up at every point with the words 'Sorry, this country is full'. What we have come to call the 'gutter press' does not change much, even in its grammar. (The gutter itself has improved more than the press which carries its name.) It has been fairly consistently one of the major factors in promoting and reinforcing racist ideas among the British people.

Opposition to immigration has included members of all major political parties. The Labour Party opposed a motion from the

Independent Labour Party (ILP) at the World Migration Conference in 1926 which objected to exclusion of people 'purely on grounds of race and colour'. Even during the Nazi regime, on 23 March 1938, the *Daily Mail* maintained its anti-immigrant stance, warning that 'the floodgates would be opened'. A few years earlier, on 4 June 1935, its proprietor, Lord Rothermere, had praised the 'hidden light' of Hitler. In the post-war period, as early as 5 November 1954, before there was significant immigration from the 'coloured Common-wealth', John Hynd, Labour MP for Sheffield Attercliffe, was calling for control of entry. In the same year, a confidential memorandum from a Home Office Working Party on *Coloured People Seeking Employment within the UK* advised the government that discrimination at employment exchanges was not practical, and that control at the point of entry was preferable. This was a foretaste of things to come.

British immigration law has not been a well-considered and systematic policy, with clear social and economic goals, but rather a series of responses to particular pressures. After the Second World War, in 1948, the first members of a new wave of Jamaican migrants arrived on the ship *Empire Windrush*. The response of the Minister of Labour, George Isaacs, speaking in the House of Commons on 8 June 1948, was significant, and an omen for the future: 'I hope no encouragement will be given to others to follow their example.'

From agitation to control: 1958–62

In the years after the Second World War there was a resurgence and revival of racist and fascist groups, though on a small and localized scale. There were outbursts of racist agitation at various points. The misleadingly named 'Notting Hill riots' of 1958 formed a significant watershed in attitudes to immigration. Looked at from our present perspective, the 'riots' seem rather insignificant and small scale, though they have been described as some of the worst outbreaks of civil unrest and racial violence in Britain in the twentieth century. But they were significant for two reasons. First, when Lord Justice Salmon sentenced the young men responsible for the attacks on West Indians, he described them as 'a minute and insignificant section of the population'. In this way the current conception of racial prejudice – the word 'racism' was not in the dictionaries at this time – was articulated. The prejudiced and violent were a deplorable blot on the otherwise tolerant and welcoming landscape of Britain, but they were statistically insignificant. Second, the immediate response from the media and some politicians, and the eventual response of the government, was not to act legislatively against racial discrimination or violence, nor to initiate educational strategies, but to control black immigration, working on what Ruth Glass termed 'the number theory of prejudice'.

The polemic – it is not accurate to call it a debate – on immigration which took place after 1958 and culminated in the passing of the Commonwealth Immigrants Act in 1962, was at first associated with fringe parliamentary figures such as Norman Pannell and Cyril Osborne, but within a short time their views had become mainstream orthodoxy. Hostility to black immigrants, combined with the need for cheap labour, created a situation where, as the Milner Holland report on London housing, commissioned by the Government after publicity in the early 1960s on housing racketeering in the capital, was to show, those who were needed in (and in some cases positively recruited for) the labour market found no foothold in the housing market. These were the years of Perec Rachman, but all this was years before Enoch Powell (whose influence will be examined later in this chapter) had uttered a word on the subject of race and immigration (though he played his part in drafting the 1957 Rent Act which exacerbated the housing rackets).

In the years prior to the 1962 legislation, immigration from the Caribbean, India and Pakistan was small. John MacGregor, later to become a Conservative minister, showed in an article in *Crossbow* (New Year 1962, pp. 45–50) that between 1946 and 1959 the percentage net immigration to Britain was as follows: Australia, Canada, New Zealand and South Africa 16.5; Eire 51.5; Other Commonwealth 8.1; India and Pakistan 6.5; British West Indies 16.5. It was only the last two categories that caused concern. Yet within days of the 1958 events, on 3 September, the *Daily Mirror* was campaigning for control of immigration. Jeffrey Hamm, Oswald Mosley's right-hand man, said that 'The *Mirror* is expressing our policy.' On the same day in the *Daily Sketch*, Hamm had said: 'I tell you the answer is to send them home. Get rid of them.' *The People* had anticipated the post-Notting Hill events. 'For their own sakes, stop them now', it proclaimed on 25 May 1958. Among early campaigners to end 'coloured immigration' were John Hynd and his fellow Labour MP George Rogers. By 1961 the calls for control had increased, while a 'beat the ban' panic had led to an unprecedented increase in immigration from India and Pakistan. The prospect of an Act to control immigration had led to the very increase it was supposed to avert! Asian people in Britain were horrified by the increasingly explicit racism of the anti-immigrant rhetoric. The Birmingham Pakistani Workers Association issued a statement in August saying that the expressions of prejudice and the practice of discrimination were part of a pattern of global racism, and were 'no different from those that led to Little Rock, Sharpeville, Notting Hill and the tragedies revealed at the Eichmann trial'.

For a while even Conservatives insisted that there must be no control based on racial discrimination. David Renton, the Home Office minister, said on 28 July 1961 that 'we could not contemplate restrictions based on race and colour'. But such noble sentiments were short lived, and the government moved towards control. The Home Secretary, R. A. Butler, in 1961 assured members of the Conservative Party that, if they gave the government time, it would find a solution which was 'not based on colour prejudice *alone*' (my italics). The Commonwealth Immigrants Bill was debated towards the end of 1961 and became law in 1962. The Labour leader, Hugh Gaitskell, in the House of Commons on 16 November 1961 said, in language which recalled that of R. H. Tawney: 'The test of a civilized country is how it behaves to all its citizens of different race, religion and colour. By that test this bill fails and that is fundamentally why we deplore it.' On 23 November he called it a 'miserable, shameful, shoddy bill', and shouted across the House, 'It is because they are coloured.' The *Guardian* editorial on 17 November was entitled 'The colour bar uncamouflaged', while *The Times* on the 14th said that the damage it would do 'can hardly be exaggerated'. The *Daily Mirror* called it 'Britain's race law'. However, it is clear that many Labour politicians, in retrospect, came to the view that the party should not have opposed the controls. Roy Hattersley, who is now, in the New Labour context, seen as very much left of centre, argued as early as 1965 that there were 'honourable reasons for restricting immigration'. He supported controls in that year, and said that the Labour Party should have done so in 1962. Another Labour MP, Brian Walden, speaking on the BBC on 2 August 1965, defended the legislation on the grounds of pressure on resources and the inability of the newcomers to integrate quickly.

In 1962 some church leaders attacked the early legislation, though in very restrained ways, while others supported it. Cardinal

Godfrey issued a Pastoral Letter on 27 May 1961 in support of controls. In contrast Archbishop Ramsey, in the House of Lords on 12 March 1962, referred to 'this Bill which is indeed deplorable', and accused the government of failing to attack the conditions which led to racial discrimination and social problems. From South London, Fr Eric James wrote of the racism of the bill, adding, 'If the Conservatives and Socialists will not say it outright, then the church must' (*South London Observer*, 9 October 1961). But the national newspaper of the Church of England, the *Church Times*, told its readers on 3 November that 'the fact that most of those affected will ' ɔ West Indians or Asian is an accident which cannot be helped', missing the obvious point that if this had not been the case, the legislation would not have been introduced. The 1962 Act was intended, in the words of its Preamble, as a 'temporary provision'. However, the legislation was tightened in 1965, and in subsequent years, until it was replaced by the Act of 1971.

The strengthening of controls

In 1964 Peter Griffiths was elected as Conservative MP for Smethwick. A major part of the local electoral campaign had been a poster proclaiming 'If you want a nigger for a neighbour, vote Labour'. At that time he was seen as an oddity, even, in Prime Minister Harold Wilson's words, as 'a parliamentary leper'. However, these years were of crucial importance. The pendulum of decency in race debate was swinging to the right, and more respectable figures were now feeling able to say openly what had previously been left to the racist groups. Philip Mason, Director of the Institute of Race Relations, wrote in the *Guardian* on 23 January 1965 that it was essential to cut down the number of immigrants 'until this mouthful has been digested'. So by this point the language had changed, and such a way of referring to human beings had become acceptable in a 'liberal' newspaper. A few days earlier Peregrine Worsthorne had said that most people wanted to keep Britain white (*Sunday Telegraph*, 17 January 1965).

Cyril Osborne, Conservative MP for Louth, was a key figure in anti-immigrant polemic during the 1960s. On 11 November 1961, in a letter to *The Economist*, he wrote: 'Do you believe the entire Commonwealth of nearly 600 million people should have the undisputed right to dump in England its criminals, its lunatics, its lepers, and its own vast unnumbered unemployed?' On the opening day of the Conservative Party conference, 18 October 1967, the *Daily Telegraph* published a letter from Osborne in which he claimed that immigration 'could destroy our race'. 'In our grandchildren's time there could well be more coloured than white people in Britain.' On 11 February 1968, in the *News of the World*, he repeated his warning. 'If we go on like this, there will be more blacks than whites here in seventy years time.'

Today many will read Osborne's words with horror and disgust. However, it should not be forgotten that, by the mid-1960s, the Labour Party had more or less adopted Osborne's view. Cabinet papers from 1965, released in May 1998, show that the Home Secretary in the Wilson government, Sir Frank Soskice, was arguing that 'the country has been taking in coloured immigrants faster than they can be assimilated', and that the government needed 'to bring the flood under control'. In January 1965 Soskice told Wilson that black immigrants were 'a social problem of increasing proportions'. The implications of this view for law were manifested in the White Paper of 1965, which has rightly been seen as the foundation document of modern racism. By introducing a quota system, this paper and the legislation which followed it established in law the number theory of racism: the view that racism was directly related to the numbers of black people. It also made permanent the 'temporary provision' of the 1962 Act. The kind of language used by Soskice was taken up by his Conservative and Labour followers. Thus Reginald Maudling in 1968 referred to the problem of the arrival in the UK of people of 'wholly alien cultures, habits and outlook' who then, presumably of their own free will, 'tend to concentrate in their own communities' (cited in Smith, 1977, p. 118). Ten years later Maudling felt able to go further and admit that immigration policy was about 'coloured' immigration. That, he said, is 'what the argument is all about'. If the legislation was racially discriminatory, he asserted, 'there is not necessarily any harm in that'. What was important was that 'we should be honest about it' (*The Times*, 13 April 1978). So, according to this view, racism was fine as long as we were honest about it! In a sense this marked a crucial turning point in the development of the political approach: it was the point at which the explicitly racist element was publicly recognized, even recognized with some degree of pride. Views which had previously been identified with the racist wing of the political parties had now become an integral part of the mainstream.

The year 1968 was crucial. In response to the Kenyan Asians issue, the British passport was devalued in that year, creating two categories of British subject. The new Commonwealth Immigrants ('Kenyan Asians') Act was rushed through parliament in 36 hours. It was this legislation which began the process that confirmed inequality in citizenship. Ruth Glass, writing to *The Times* on 26 February 1968, argued that 'if the immigration Bill is passed, the Race Relations Bill is cancelled out in advance', while the following day in the same paper Peter Calvocoressi said that 'racism is to be written into British law'. On the same day, in an editorial, *The Times* called it 'the most shameful measure that Labour members have ever been asked by their whips to support'. It introduced the idea, and made it a reality, that a passport was valid if the holder was white, and not valid if she or he was black. So two types of British citizen emerged: those who were 'ancestral', and the rest. It was condemned by the International Commission of Jurists and by the European Court of Human Rights. But it formed the basis of future legislation, particularly the Immigration Act of 1971. This Act established the concept of 'patriality' by which persons with parents or grandparents born in Britain were privileged over others. Inevitably the majority of these persons were white, but government apologists at the time claimed that this was merely an accident of history.

The coming to power of Margaret Thatcher in 1979 did further enormous damage to race relations in the UK. Indeed the country has probably never recovered from this. Mrs Thatcher's notorious television interview of January 1978 is mainly remembered for its introduction of the concept of 'swamping' by people of an 'alien culture'. In the same interview she stressed the importance of allaying fears about numbers. At the General Election of 1979, in every area where the National Front had shown signs of success, their vote collapsed and there was a massive swing to the Conservatives. In London constituencies the swing was 14 per cent in Barking, 11.6 per cent in Hackney South and 10.8 per cent in Islington Central.

The Thatcher years saw the erosion of citizenship rights in the British Nationality Act of 1981, and tighter controls, expressed particularly in the Immigration Act of 1988. This Act removed the right of those settled before 1973 to bring in wives and children, made overstaying a continuing offence, and restricted the right of appeal against deportation. But it was clear, in this period, that immigration officers had little education on human rights issues; decisions were often arbitrary, and against the UN Convention on Refugees of 1951. In January 1989, when Viraj Mendis was deported from Manchester to Sri Lanka, there had been 584 political deaths in Sri Lanka. There was no improvement in ensuing years. The 1996 Act made matters worse, and effectively employers were forced to act as agents of the Home Office, criminalized if they employed undocumented workers.

The election of the 'New Labour' government in 1997 seemed full of hope, but in many respects it has continued Thatcherite policies, while in others it has made the Conservatives seem quite liberal. Benefits were removed by the Asylum and Immigration Act 1999, which established a system of vouchers. Today figures from the Thatcher years like Michael Heseltine seem positively left wing, so far has the pendulum swung. The 1999 Act has been criticized for its discrimination against poor people through its insistence on financial securities, its removal of right of appeal, and its failure to respect the fact that many genuine refugees have no way of providing acceptable documents. On more than one occasion the House of Lords has pointed to the fact that changes in immigration legislation are in conflict with the European Convention on Human Rights. But this is typical of the immigration legislation as a whole.

The Nationality, Immigration and Asylum Act 2002 confined asylum seekers to certain centres and denied mainstream education to their children. This Act was preceded by the White Paper *Secure Borders, Safe Havens*, a document apparently based on economic nationalism and a racialized notion of citizenship. It sought both to keep out unwanted labour and to control access to citizenship. The insistence on confinement was based on a policy of exclusion with the likelihood that expulsion would follow as the logical consequence. The insistence on valid passports or identity documents ignores the fact that many who flee persecution cannot obtain these. Section 55 of the Act removed the right to state benefits and housing unless the individual had made a claim for asylum within 24 hours of arrival. Like previous Acts, this too created real distress. The Home Affairs Select Committee in January 2004 rightly called the legislation 'unduly harsh', pointing out that at least half of asylum seekers were fleeing conflict. A 2004 study entitled *Destruction by Design*, undertaken on behalf of the Mayor of London, Ken

Livingstone, claimed that 10,000 asylum seekers had been made destitute by the legislation, producing a level of distress 'not seen in the capital for generations'.

Health and social services have become increasingly involved in policing. At the time of writing, identity cards are under discussion. (Interestingly, this is not a new notion. Under the Aliens Restriction Amendment Act of 1919, non-British people were obliged to carry identity cards and notify the authorities if they were away for two weeks. The *Jewish Chronicle* on 30 May 1919 called this a 'war on aliens'.) It is noteworthy that, in a parliamentary answer on 5 February 2000, David Blunkett used the term 'universal entitlement cards', indicating that the underlying purpose was not simply identity but rights to benefits. A linked issue also currently under both discussion and experimentation is that of citizenship tests and ceremonies of British culture. And running through the whole debate is the rhetoric of exclusion, expulsion, designated centres, special education, and so on. Clearly the idea of 'social inclusion', a theme which has been central to New Labour thinking, has boundaries, and immigrants are often beyond those boundaries.

There have been continuing and growing protests at the inhumanity of the legislation. However, less attention has been given to the theoretical basis of immigration control.

The ideology of immigration control

The polemic of 1958–62 was marked by two related assumptions: that prejudice was inevitable and therefore some compromise with it was needed, and that the incidence of prejudice was directly related to numbers. The number theory, linked with the unexamined notion that racial discrimination at the doors of the UK was the best way to reduce racial prejudice within the country, was to form the basis of British 'firm but fair' policy for years to come. The years from 1958 to 1971 were crucial, and the White Paper of 1965, which explicitly made race the determining factor in numerical control, has been correctly described (by Robert Moore) as 'the foundation document in the history of contemporary racism' (*Guardian*, 16 April 1988).

Paragraph 8.1 of the White Paper *Fairer, Faster and Firmer*, issued in 1998 – the very title was an example of jargon aimed at mystification – claimed that 'the UK government has a long-standing tradition of giving shelter to those fleeing persecution'. But this is naïve, simplistic and historically inaccurate. Between 1933 and 1939, Britain admitted 55,000 refugees from Nazism, refusing more. The *Daily Mail* described even this action as 'misguided sentimentalism'.

To claim that there has been an 'ideology' behind immigration control is perhaps to allow more intellectual credibility than is deserved. It has rather been a series of crude and unexamined assumptions, supported and reinforced by a series of simple-minded clichés – firm but fair, tough and tender, and the like. The basic assumption is that there is a direct link between numbers and prejudice. The more black people, the greater the problems. This proposition has been repeated *ad nauseam* by politicians of both major parties as if it were so obvious that there was no need to demonstrate its truth. Sir Alec Douglas-Home, Prime Minister in the 1960s, claimed that 'integration . . . would never be achieved unless the strictest limitation was applied' (*Guardian*, 4 February 1965), while Roy Hattersley similarly said: 'Without integration, limitation is inexcusable: without limitation, integration is impossible' (cited Deakin, 1970, p. 106). Maurice Foley, the Labour minister responsible for Commonwealth immigration in the Wilson era, went so far as to claim, on 9 October 1965, that 'the situation was bound to worsen as the number of coloured people increased'. On 14 May 1984, David Waddington, then the Minister for Immigration, said that immigration control should be 'firm and fair', and that such control was 'not inimical to good community relations but an essential part of them' (*Guardian*, 14 May 1984). Home Secretary Douglas Hurd in 1989 repeated the message. We were, he said, building greater harmony, but 'success in that task depends on maintaining firm but fair immigration control' (*Independent*, 26 July 1989). Thirty years later Michael Howard, then Home Secretary, assured readers of the *Daily Telegraph* on 22 May 1995 that 'firm and fair immigration control has always been at the heart of good race relations'. Howard made the same point on his well-publicized visit to Burnley in February 2004 where he condemned the British National Party but insisted on the Conservatives' commitment to immigration control. The term 'firm but fair' has become one of the many clichés – substitutes for thought – which have marked British politics in the last few decades.

Throughout the rhetoric, there were some who admitted that colour was at the heart of the demands for control. Some, such as the Conservative MPs Cyril Osborne and, later, Enoch Powell, were entirely open about it, while others were more equivocal. Osborne saw race as an insoluble issue. Racial problems had not been solved anywhere in the world, he claimed in *The Observer* on 22 October 1961, and it would be 'the height of folly' to import them to Britain. The theory is simple. Racism only arises where there are black people to produce it. Therefore if there are fewer blacks, there will be less racism. If there are no blacks at all, racism will disappear.

By 1965 support for immigration control was coming from what might have seemed unexpected quarters. In an extraordinary article in the *Guardian* in 1965, Philip Mason, director of the Institute of Race Relations, referred to areas in which over 20 per cent of the population were (black) immigrants (though the 1961 Census had shown that there were few enumeration districts in which black people formed more than 15 per cent). In the months prior to the 1965 White Paper, Mason was advising the National Committee for Commonwealth Immigrants not to become a spokesman or champion of the immigrants as against the rest of the community.

The debate became more heated and hysterical with the intervention, after 1968, of Enoch Powell, for many years a Conservative MP. Powell was a key figure in making racism respectable in Britain. Almost uniquely among political figures who were not prime ministers, he has the distinction of giving birth to a noun, 'Powellism'. His inflammatory speeches, delivered over a number of years, gave credibility to what many people had been saying or thinking. In a talk given at St Anne's Church, Soho, on 14 October 1968, the youth worker Geof Bevan, based in North Kensington, expressed what many of us were feeling: 'Enoch Powell has done inestimable damage by giving a whole lot of confidence to racially prejudiced white people: they now feel they are right.' Powell, writing on 20 April 1993, the 25th anniversary of the 'rivers of blood' speech, still believed that events had confirmed his thesis, and *The Times* gave him a platform to say so.

Powell was an interesting figure, highly intelligent, with an academic background in ancient Greek. This was both an advantage and a hindrance. He always saw, and latched on to, the iota subscripts, the fine detail, but often missed the central point of the argument. He was extremely clever at focusing a debate on minutiae, but there was an air of unreality about him which often created a world of illusion in which he believed he spoke for the 'man in the street'. While he was often ridiculed as 'yesterday's man', he, more than any other individual, helped to make racism respectable. From 1968 onwards, it was clear from his correspondence that there was significant support for his views among white people. After one speech he received 110,000 letters of which only 2,030 were hostile (Spearman, 1968, 1969). From observing his behaviour, from personal correspondence, and from witnessing the impact of his speeches, I believe that he never understood the evil consequences of his work. Trying to communicate these to him was a lost cause. In many ways he was a sad and tragic figure, but the harm he did remains with us.

Yet I do not believe that Powell was racist in the usual sense of being a believer in racial discrimination, a fact to which a number of his black constituents in Wolverhampton have testified. On 10 October 1965 he wrote:

> I have set and will always set my face like flint against making any difference between one citizen of this country and another on grounds of his origin. I am certain that not only the Conservative Party but the overwhelming majority of people in this country are of the same mind, and wish to see coloured immigrants integrated into the life and society of what is now their homeland. (Cited in Foot, 1969, p. 66.)

Powell held that black immigrants were 'detachments of communities in the West Indies or India and Pakistan encamped in certain areas of England' (Powell, 1969, p. 311). He coined the phrase 'the alien wedge' (*The Times,* 19 July 1969) which was later to be used by the defenders of Thatcherism. 'These people must recognize that they are aliens', he told the German magazine *Der Spiegel* in 1978. Peregrine Worsthorne has claimed that what we came to call Thatcherism was once called Powellism. In 1984 Powell criticized the Queen for her Christmas broadcast, accusing her of showing more sympathy to immigrants and foreigners than to her 'own people'. She was 'more concerned for the susceptibilities and prejudices of a vociferous minority of newcomers than for the great mass of her subjects'. Interestingly, by 2003, the Office of National Statistics was reporting that non-whites were more likely to call themselves British than were members of the white population (*Financial Times*, 15 March 2003).

The apocalyptic language employed by Powell had been used earlier by Cyril Osborne, as well as by the openly racist groups of whom Powell disapproved but to whom he gave both ammunition and credibility. 'In fifteen or twenty years' time', he predicted in his 'rivers of blood' speech, 'the black man will hold the whip over the white man'. Britain was no longer the same nation, he claimed in 1985, and perhaps not a nation at all.

In the UK the rhetoric around immigration has for many years been characterized by words such as 'swamping'. Inherited from Margaret Thatcher in the 1970s, and later used by Labour politician David Blunkett, the word frequently appeared at local level. In 1993 a Labour candidate in East London commented that in the mornings his area was 'swamped with Bangladeshis trying to get to school'. The dramatic and inflammatory language used by Powell was used by many less significant and less intelligent figures. Thus Winston Churchill (junior) spoke in 1993 of the 'relentless flood', and of the threat to the 'British way of life', claiming that the population of many northern cities was 'well over 50 per cent immigrant'. Even the Conservative leader in the Welsh Assembly used the word 'swamped' in 2003 although asylum seekers in Wales formed only 0.7 per cent of the population.

A study of press coverage in 1992 was fairly typical. It included headlines about bogus refugees – 'madness on migrants', 'London will be swamped by refugees', and 'the spectre of mass immigration'. The Runnymede Trust carried out a further study of over 6,500 press cuttings on immigration in June 2001, and concluded that they were 'mostly negative'.

Throughout the recent political rhetoric, as was the case in its earlier forms, there has been an assumption that refugees, asylum seekers and most immigrants (unless they happen to meet the current needs of the global market) are intrinsically undesirable and problematic. Beverley Hughes, a key figure within the New Labour government until her resignation in 2004, made a revealing statement on 12 June 2002. The problems of immigration, she claimed, were highlighted by 'Dutch nationals of Somali descent'. Between 2,000 and 10,000 people of Somali origin, she said, had come to Leicester in eighteen months. So the 'problem' was not just numbers but the fact that the immigrants were Somali or of Somali descent.

More recently, the same arguments have resurfaced in a more intellectual, liberal and gentrified form. Thus the (former Marxist) economist Bob Rowthorn wrote in *Prospect* in February 2003 about the way in which large numbers of immigrants made the sense of a 'coherent national history' more difficult, and were a 'threat to national cohesion'.

Not surprisingly, in such a climate, political figures, journalists and others have increasingly felt free to make the racial basis of their concern explicit, rather than hiding it beneath the rhetoric of 'numbers not colour'. Thus Charles Moore, writing in *The Spectator* on 19 October 1991, argued for the encouragement of immigrants from Europe, but not 'Muslims and blacks'. He favoured a 'more liberal and "racist"' immigration policy. Roy Jenkins, who had played a key role in the race legislation, told the *Independent* Magazine (4 March 1985) that, in retrospect, he believed that more caution should have been exercised to avoid the creation of substantial Muslim communities.

Sadly, but predictably, it is not at all clear where the British government stands on this critical issue. Appeasement has undoubtedly been the norm in the Labour Party since immigration controls began in 1962. It is not clear that 'New Labour' is new at this point: the immigration service is exempt from the provisions of the Race Relations (Amendment) Act of 2000 relating to discrimination in public places.

Ruth Glass put it forcefully in 1969:

Were there no racial conflicts in the United States before the 10 per cent black mark was reached? Would harmony be established if half or more of the American black population went away? We had racial disturbances in Britain at various periods – from 1919 in Cardiff and Liverpool to 1958 in Nottingham and Notting Hill when there were only a few coloured people here. The Jewish segment of the German population was one per cent when Hitler decided that zero per cent should be the final solution. (Letter in *The Times*, 4 August 1969)

In an earlier letter she had described the demands for tighter and tighter controls as 'a new doctrine of original sin together with a new faulty political arithmetic' (*The Times*, 5 August 1967).

The churches have, particularly since the 1980s, realized that the core of immigration policy in Europe is the assumption of the dispensability of human life. The 1999 Asylum and Immigration Act met with strong opposition from the churches, and local churches are now heavily involved in feeding and supporting many refugees and asylum seekers who have been deprived of state benefits. The churches' role as advocates for the scapegoats and victims of racist immigration policies will become more important in the coming years, and Christians will need to cooperate closely with people of other faiths, particularly Muslims, who in many cases will be the victims of the legislation.

Opposition to racism within the immigration system has been increasing among the British churches at national as well as local level, and this has continued under New Labour as they have continued and extended the policies of Thatcher and her successors.

The global dimensions of migration

On 22 January 1971 the Commonwealth Heads of Government produced a Declaration of Commonwealth Principles. It included the assertion that no country of the Commonwealth would cooperate with 'regimes which practise racial discrimination'. If this were taken seriously, the Commonwealth countries would have ceased to cooperate with Britain over thirty years ago.

However, today, the effects of wars and revolutions, of poverty and economic hardship, of persecution and changes in the global economy, have made international migration a central part of human life and work. The world of settled, static communities with clear boundaries has gone for ever. In European countries, foreign-born populations have grown since 1950. By 1992, that of Germany had grown from 1.1 to 8.6 per cent, that of Luxembourg from 9.8 to 29.1 per cent, that of Belgium from 4.1 to 9.1 per cent and that of Holland from 1 to 5.1 per cent. Paris is now the second largest Portuguese city in the world, while in Switzerland, foreign-born residents account for over 16 per cent of the population.

In North America, Los Angeles is home to over 400,000 El Salvadorians, and David Rieff has called it the capital of the Third World. There are more Salvadorians in Los Angeles than there are in San Salvador. By 1998 Latinos had outnumbered 'Anglos' in Los Angeles County. In New York, the Bronx area witnessed an increase of 87.8 per cent in its population of East Asian origin between 1980 and 1990, while Hispanics increased by 32.4 per cent. There are now estimated to be 32 million Latinos in the US and this may increase to 59 million by 2025. By 2050 it is estimated that Latinos will outnumber black Americans. The Latino presence has already led to a significant transformation of urban space (13).

One worrying feature of recent years has been the increased flow of persons without any roots in communities, dependent on industries without any clear liabilities. In this context, the question of democratic citizenship becomes essential if individuals are not to become simply e-mail addresses and their attachments to a location brief and superficial. Churches and other groups have come to see the need to organize, and to campaign with and for, the vast numbers of low paid migrant workers who are extremely vulnerable.

One of the myths perpetrated in the immigration debate is that immigrants are bad for the economy. In 1989, during the controversy about the status of residents of Hong Kong, the economist Bernard Corry pointed out that immigration to Britain from Hong Kong would lead to faster economic growth particularly in the construction industry and computer electronics, and that the benefits would outweigh the costs. Even if all the immigrants settled in the south-east of England, he claimed, a 3p rise in income tax would cover the cost (*South China Morning Post*, 2 July 1989). The Hong Kong debate was interesting. While David Waddington, a government minister at the time, was worried that an obligation to take all five million inhabitants of Hong Kong would lead to an 'Armageddon situation', others recognized that migrants from Hong Kong were likely to be highly skilled. By the 1990s a Home Office study, *The Settlement of Refugees in Britain* (1995), showed that many recent asylum seekers were very highly qualified.

The link between immigration and unemployment is another area which is often misunderstood. In the US, immigration reached its highest level between 1900 and 1925 – a period which included the First World War and the Great Depression – when unemployment was 5.05 per cent. During the following seventy years immigration fell and unemployment rose. The work of the British geographer Ceri Peach on West Indian migration to the UK has shown that migration followed employment needs closely. As in the US in the earlier period, immigration levels fell as unemployment increased. On the other hand, economic success invariably leads to increased immigration. Investment bankers earn more in London than in New York, so it is not surprising to find that there are around 250,000 non-national professionals in London and the south-east of England, probably the largest concentration of such persons in the world. A recent study for the Home Office by University College, London showed, as had earlier studies, that immigration tends to boost, rather than depress, general wage levels.

In the coming years immigration will become a major issue in many more countries. It has been estimated that between 2004 and 2034, 90 per cent of the additions to the world's labour force will be in the 'developing' countries, and most literate workers will be there. Christian and other 'faith communities' will have a major task in trying to develop a rational and humane debate on the issue, in combating racism and hysteria in immigration policy and rhetoric, and in providing support for the victims of these policies. It will be an uphill struggle, and, to change the metaphor, Christians and people of goodwill will find themselves swimming against the tide. They will find themselves making alliances in unlikely places, and will encounter much opposition within the ranks of the churches. Yet how immigrants, asylum seekers and refugees are treated is a real test of our humanity and our commitment to justice.

On 28 January 1948 an aircraft crashed in Los Gatos Canyon in Mexico, killing all on board, including 28 Mexicans who had been deported from the US. When a newscaster reported that they were 'just deportees', that comment led to Woody Guthrie's famous song 'Deportees'. For nothing exposes so clearly what Hannah Arendt called 'the banality of evil' as does the practice of immigration control. It is evil because it divides families, excludes refugees, detains people who have committed no offence, and forcibly deports others. It treats human beings as if they were disposable refuse. While it is not fascism, it is 'certainly a step towards fascism' (Cohen, 2004, p. 16). Resistance by Christians to current immigration policy is not an eccentric political posture: it is a resistance to the dehumanizing of the children of God.

4 | The Birth of a Monster: racial conflict and local experience

It would not occur to anyone who writes a book on criminology to state in the preface that he is opposed to murder.
(Ruth Glass (1960, p. xi))

Certainly it is not the respectable propagandists of colour quotas who scrawl 'Nigger go home' slogans on the walls of back alleys. But they produce a doctrine of white Malthusianism which may well encourage others to do so.
(Ruth Glass, letter in *The Times*, 4 August 1969)

Racially motivated violence occurs throughout the world. There are conflicts between black and white, between tribal groups of the same colour, between Hindus and Muslims, between blacks and Jews, between people of the same colour and religion but of different ethnic origin, and so on. There are attacks by members of majority communities on minorities, as well as, for example in apartheid South Africa, by minorities on the majority. Much racial violence is structural, legislated and enforced by state officials. More commonly, it is encouraged and given respectability by the current political climate. Although, historically, most racial violence has been perpetrated by white people, the dominant group globally, against black and other groups, this is no longer the whole story. Increasingly, white minorities in some countries are targeted, while religious minorities, whether Christian, Jewish, Muslim or whatever, may be the victims of sustained attack. On a global scale, the recent – and, as I write, ongoing – wars against Iraq have increased the incidence of racial violence, specifically attacks on Muslims in Britain, the US and elsewhere, but also, in some countries, on white people who are identified, rightly or wrongly, with anti-Muslim foreign policy. Global policies are directly linked to local street violence against individuals, yet another example of what some sociologists call the 'glocal'.

And, of course, in many places, violence is within, not between, ethnic groups. On 2 February 1990 the *Chicago Reporter* pointed out that 'black youth are city's top murder risk', but said that most of the murders were by other black people. In the US, right-wing paramilitary groups such as the World Church of the Creator have been associated with the fire-bombing of synagogues, and there is abundant evidence that similar groups remain active in many states. Such groups as the Aryan Nation, the Michigan Militia and the Christian Identity movement believe in organized violence to defend the white Christian order. In Britain, many young people have been attacked simply because of their Muslim names. Thus 13-year-old Aklamah Hussein was attacked by boys from his own school in Manchester in 1991, a clear example again of the 'glocal', the way in which the global affects the local.

At least two false conclusions can be drawn from these data. The first is that inter-racial conflict is inevitable, part of 'human nature' or of 'the system', and that the only response is to keep the 'races' apart. Apart from the fact that such a response is impossible even if it were desirable, there is nothing inevitable here. In a radio discussion in 1981, Lord Scarman, one of our more liberal judges, observed that, while black and white individuals often got on well together, when they were driven into groups the 'herd instinct' took over, and trouble began. The implication was that this was an inevitable process. The idea of 'historical inevitability' is a dangerous doctrine and leads to inaction, complacency and paralysis. But, in my view, it is also politically disastrous. Like the manifestation of anger at the personal level, the appearance of inter-racial conflict is a warning sign that something is wrong and must be tackled.

The second false conclusion is that inter-racial conflicts are temporary aberrations, and that the most appropriate response is to do nothing, to react calmly and carry on as before. There is an element of truth in this claim since instant, impulsive and unreflective reactions can make situations worse. But 'leave well alone' is not a wise maxim in the area of work for justice. This is not to say that sometimes to do nothing may not be a wise political strategy. Pharmacologists know that, in cases of adverse reactions to drugs, inaction can sometimes be the swiftest healer. But inaction needs to be a positive strategy, not a euphemism for laziness.

In this chapter I shall focus mainly on one small area, the East End of London, though I hope that what I say will be relevant to situations elsewhere.

I arrived in London for the first time, aged 19, in the autumn of 1958, just after the 'Notting Hill riots' had occurred. (Like many disturbances, they have acquired a misleading name, for they were not strictly riots but a series of attacks by white youths on West Indians, and they did not occur in Notting Hill but rather in Notting Dale, Shepherd's Bush and Kensal Town.) The impact of these incidents was being felt in other parts of London, and 'Keep Britain White' signs and swastikas had begun to appear on walls in the East End and elsewhere. Racial violence was again becoming respectable.

Early racial conflicts

I say 'again' because, while each generation seems to have to learn lessons as if for the first time, racial conflict was not new to London, or new at all. Conflicts occur from time to time between groups who differ according to national origin, skin colour, religion, language, and a wide range of other characteristics. The absence of conflict is also common: groups all over the world have often lived together amicably in spite of such differences. Wider economic, political and social events can affect how groups in a small area relate to one another. Neither harmony nor conflict are fixed entities: they are neither inevitable nor, once they have arisen, easily resolved. Similarly, a high degree of prejudice in a population does not necessarily lead to racial conflict or violence: what may be more important, as Ruth Glass pointed out, reflecting on the events of 1958, is the absence of positive forces working in the opposite direction.

I shall now examine these issues in the East End of London, and, in this context, I shall consider three factors: the historical relationships between different communities; the appearance of inter-racial violence; and the role of organized racist movements in exploiting situations of anxiety, frustration and fear.

The East End of London is one of the most racially mixed areas in Britain. It has been a diverse area for centuries, and many writers have claimed that it offers a model of mutual tolerance and harmony for other communities. Certainly there are many examples of friendship, cooperation and good working relationships, for instance, those between Irish Roman Catholic and Jewish groups in the 1930s. Today relations between white and Bengali people here are probably better than in many parts of Britain. There have been many mixed race marriages, and considerable mingling in the pubs, shops and schools. However, East End history is filled with examples of racial conflict, in most cases inflamed and aggravated by organized 'hate groups'.

Attacks on individuals and groups, on the basis of their colour, language, style of dress or perceived characteristics, have been common throughout history. The roots of such attacks are often referred to by the word 'xenophobia', fear of strangers. Colour is a key factor, but not the only one. It is not uncommon for people of virtually identical skin colour to be involved in violent conflicts which may be based on religion, national histories, language, lifestyle, sexual orientation (actual or believed), real or alleged conflicts over resources, and so on.

These kinds of conflict must not be ignored, but they are not in the strict sense racial. A racial conflict is one in which the idea of 'race' and the reality of colour are central to the conflict. In Britain, the very fact of having a black or brown face, irrespective of one's geographical origin or religion, is often the key factor in violence. This is something which many white people fail to understand. White people may hold strong anti-racist opinions and have impeccable records of action on controversial matters. Black people are instantly recognized by their faces, and are thus far more vulnerable.

It was in East London that the term 'Paki-bashing' arose. The victims of attack were people who, by their looks, were believed to be Pakistani: whether they did originate in Pakistan was irrelevant. Skin colour was the key factor. The term 'Paki-bashing' seems to have been first used on the Collingwood Estate in Bethnal Green in 1969, and it was followed within weeks by the first use of the word 'skinhead', now a term used from North America to Russia. At this stage, although the first post-war fascist party, the National Front (NF), had been formed, most of the violence seems not to have been organized by any political group, though the speeches of Enoch Powell from 1968 onwards undoubtedly gave it a certain respectability.

In 1978, when both the fascist organizing and the resistance to it in the East End reached its peak, there was a massive increase in racially motivated violence. Of course, not all of this was the direct result of fascist activity, but they had given the green light to it and created an atmosphere in which it was tolerable. Several pubs became gathering places for members of racist groups. One pub in Shoreditch was used on 20 April for the celebration of Hitler's birthday, and some of the early paramilitary groups, such as Column 88, used to gather here. They contributed to an atmosphere of fear and insecurity in the area. Not only were black and Asian people affected by this, but also students, young men with long hair, people who were, or 'looked', gay or left wing – in fact anyone who did not conform to the fascist idea of what a good patriotic Britisher should look like: white, thuggish, short-haired and wearing large boots.

A major turning point in the East End experience occurred when the Bengali community refused to accept the label of helpless victim, and became an organized political force. Like the North Africans in Paris, there was a time when most Bengalis in London did not vote. Today half of the local council in the East End are Bengali. The Bengali youth in particular 'came of age' politically in those terrible years of organized fascism. It was their radicalization and mobilization, combined with the work of the (mainly white) Anti-Nazi League, that drove the fascists out of the area, and made their presence and their rhetoric disreputable, if only for a time. The year 1978 was a turning point: it did not get rid of racist and fascist groups, but it did begin to change the climate, a factor to which I shall return in the next chapter.

The role of organized racism from Mosley to the BNP

The rise of racially motivated violence is, on the historical evidence, linked with the activity of racist organizations. However, we need to take care here. It is certainly not true that all racial attacks are committed by members of such, or indeed any, organizations. Their role is to help to mobilize, organize and encourage attacks, and to give them credibility, while from time to time distancing themselves from the violence. As Richard Edmonds of the British National Party expressed it in 1993, 'There is a lot of anger building up, and we aim to canalize it.' Earlier, another fascist activist had said, 'We have not invented racial hatred. We are organizing it.'

But the violence is often directly connected with these groups, as the criminal records of members of racist organizations show. Such organizations tend to attract individuals with a propensity for violence, a history of violent activity, and, in many cases, serious mental health problems which can be directed in violent routes.

There are questions relating to history and geography. Once the presence of racist groups in an area becomes accepted, it becomes difficult to 'decontaminate' the area. Certain locations tend to be used from one generation to another – street corners, pubs, and so on. On one occasion in the 1970s I sprinkled holy water around the National Front 'pitch' in Bethnal Green Road, and performed a liturgy of exorcism – which was much appreciated by some of my Bengali Muslim friends!

In the East End there is a long history of racist abuse. Arnold White at the end of the nineteenth century was, in his anti-Jewish polemic, very similar in style to some recent figures. So was that unpleasant character the Revd S. G. Reaney, who figured in the anti-aliens agitation of those years and wrote in the volume, edited by White, called *The Destitute Alien in Great Britain* (1892). According to Reaney,

> before we are prepared to receive the motley multitude that comes from over the sea, and across the vast plains of Russia, with open arms, as political exiles, and as religious refugees suffering from high, noble and exalted virtues, for faithfulness to the faith of their fathers and to their God, we must know more about them, and we must assure ourselves that the only reason for their expulsion from Russia is because they are so pure and saintly and true to the best traditions of the remarkable race to which they belong . . .

Reaney went on to say that at times,

> those who live and labour in the great East End feel hot and angry at the sight of the faces so un-English and the sound of the speech so utterly foreign, which crowd pavement and road on Whitechapel Waste, about the Minories, and all away down Commercial Street and Bethnal Green . . . In face, instinct, language and character their children are aliens, and still exiles. They seldom really become citizens . . .

Reaney concluded his reflections by expressing surprise that 'the depression has not turned to anger and that we have not had a "Jew-hunt" such as has been known abroad'.

The first recorded public meeting to mobilize opposition to 'alien immigration' took place at Mile End on 19 April 1887, and was chaired by Arnold White who was to figure prominently in the subsequent polemic. During these years the claim that immigrants had 'taken over' Whitechapel, and that an 'alien invasion' had occurred, was heard from many quarters. Sir William Marriott, Conservative MP for Brighton, commented in 1893 that 'there are some streets [in Whitechapel] you may go through and hardly know that you are in England'.

Similar groups have been present at many such outbreaks in the twentieth century. The link between racist and fascist groups and racial violence is well documented from the 1930s onwards in East London. It has always been denied by the groups themselves, who usually claim that they are simply articulating and expressing public resentment, and that they have not encouraged violence. But this is simple mystification. The language and the violence associated with these groups without exception leads to an increase in unrest and violence within such areas.

In the 1930s Sir Oswald Mosley and the British Union of Fascists (BUF) created a reign of terror in East London. Their target was the Jewish community, originating in Eastern Europe, and they gained considerable support in areas adjacent to the Jewish quarter of Whitechapel, particularly in Stepney, Bethnal Green and Shoreditch. It is important to note that the fascists always campaigned in these adjacent, mainly white areas, and particularly in districts of low mobility, along with strong kinship patterns, high levels of deprivation, and suspicion of 'aliens' and 'strangers'. So the National Front targeted Margate in 2000, an area with 7.2 per cent unemployment, three times the average for the south-east. This is still the case today, as the recent successes of the BNP have shown.

Mosley was still active in East London after the Second World War. He spoke outside my flat in Hoxton during the General Election campaign in 1965. But the future was to be with newer groups:

There is a tremendous vacuum in Britain at the present time into which could step a serious and responsible looking movement, adhering to the essential principles of Fascism and Nazism, but presenting them in a manner which Britons could identify with the cause of their own country as Germans and Italians a generation before.

These words were written in 1965 by John Tyndall, later to become the leader of the BNP. I was ordained priest that year, and remember Tyndall and his colleagues very well from my years as a curate in Hoxton, which became one of the strongholds of the post-war fascist parties. In the second half of the 1970s the National Front, formed in 1966–7 as the first significant post-war fascist movement, gained considerable support in almost exactly the same districts of East London in which Mosley had been successful.

The first group to use the name British National Party, led by John Bean, was one of those absorbed into the NF in 1966–7. John Tyndall, the former leader ('Führer' as he was often known in BNP circles) of the present BNP, had already left and formed the Greater Britain Movement (GBM), which joined the NF in 1967. From then onwards Tyndall and Martin Webster were the two leading figures in the NF, which quickly became the biggest post-war fascist group and which had a strong foundation in Hoxton and the East End. It was active in the East End particularly during the 1970s. The NF was a curious amalgam of several groups – Nazi, old-fashioned Tory imperialist (represented by the League of Empire Loyalists, one of the groups which helped to form the NF), and racial fundamentalist Christian – which had little in common except their hostility to black people, and many predicted its eventual disintegration as divisions became clearer. When these surfaced, they revealed inherent conflicts – around class, crime, homosexuality, interpretations of fascism, and strategy, as well as questions of personal pathology.

The main target of the new group, as far as the East End was concerned, was the Bengali community, at that time already heavily concentrated in the Brick Lane district. When I was a parish priest in Bethnal Green in the 1970s, many of the members of the 'young National Front' were children from our parish primary school. The NF had given them an identity and offered them a sense, albeit illusory, of the heroic. We need always to understand the appeal of fascism to people who feel betrayed, bored, and hopeless about the political system, something that George Orwell understood very well. Many of these young people had been rejected or abandoned by the churches, conventional youth clubs, police and probation officers, and sometimes by their own parents. The NF told them, 'You are important. We can use you.'

After the decline of the NF following the General Election of 1979 when their vote collapsed virtually everywhere, there was a fragmentation and regrouping within British fascism. The collapse of the NF vote was connected with a massive swing to the Conservatives in all the areas where they had been successful. The NF split into various groups, one of which, led by Tyndall, was originally called the New National Front. In April 1982 it became the new version of the BNP, and some members of two earlier fascist groups, the British Movement and the British Democratic Party, joined it. It took with it the journal *Spearhead*, which had previously been linked with the NF, and before that with the GBM.

The BNP, which attained national notoriety in 2004 in areas not previously associated with it in most people's minds, is the third body to carry this name since the 1960s. The first, led by John Bean (who seems still, in his old age, to be part of the new BNP), was the result of a merger of the White Defence League (WDL) and the National Labour Party (NLP) in 1960. The WDL had been active in the Notting Hill area at the time of the 1958 disturbances. The NLP was active in East London at the end of the 1950s; its East London branch had been formed at the Carpenter's Arms, Cheshire Street, Bethnal Green on 29 May 1958. The BNP used to sell their newspaper *Combat* at the corner of Cheshire Street and Kerbela Street, Bethnal Green, during the early 1960s. I remember them well, and used to attend their meetings. Bean stood in Southall at the 1964 General Election and got 9 per cent of the vote. There was a second group called the BNP, based in Leeds and led by Eddy Morrison. This group flourished in the 1970s and published *BNP Bulletin* and *British News*. It folded in 1978 and its members were urged to join the NF. The third incarnation of the BNP continues to this day and has grown in strength and, to some degree, in political sophistication. Its candidate Derek Beackon won a seat in the by-election in Millwall Ward, Isle of Dogs, on 16 September 1993, becoming the first BNP councillor in Britain, though he subsequently lost the seat at the election of 5 May 1994.

The defeat of Beackon was the result of an alliance between the Christian churches, the Samuda Women's Centre, the Bengali Action Group and the trade unions. The role of the churches was extremely important. From the moment that Beackon was elected, it was decided that a community worker would be employed with the express object of undermining the roots of the fascist vote. Through the help of the Joseph Rowntree Charitable Trust, Sue Mayo was appointed, and her role in the defeat of the BNP was of critical importance. It was a major example of a local parish acting in an analytic and a prophetic way.

A study of reactions to Beackon's election is illuminating. Some saw it as an aberration. An editorial in *The Times* on 18 September 1993, for example, stressed that it was 'not to be seen as the first stirring of an ugly racist behemoth'. It was unusual and temporary. The distinguished historian Robert Skidelsky, biographer of Mosley, explained that the East End was the only part of the UK where racist politics could have emerged. The Isle of Dogs, he said, was 'a sequestered ghetto of urban despair'. How wrong they were becomes depressingly clear as we reflect on the subsequent successes of the BNP in other areas outside London. Out of ghettoes of despair, anger often erupts.

Beackon seemed to try to exploit his populist appeal by playing on his 'ordinary bloke' image, and even on his stupidity. He once commented that he found the council 'paperwork' difficult, probably hoping that this would endear him to others who were equally confused by bureaucracy, though it is likely to have made many lose confidence in his ability to help them. At the Lansbury Ward by-election in December 1994, he called himself 'Del', apparently trying to associate himself with the lovable rogue 'Del Boy' from the TV programme *Only Fools and Horses*.

Nevertheless, at the local elections on the Isle of Dogs in May 1994, while the BNP were defeated, their three candidates did well, obtaining 9 per cent, 10.35 per cent and 8.69 per cent of the poll. What defeated them, as I shall emphasize in the next chapter, was the massive increase in the numbers of voters.

I referred above to the claim that there is now greater 'sophistication' among racist groups and particularly in the BNP. Well-informed observers have noted this change, and it is certainly true that the appeal of this group has shown more insight and 'street credibility' than it once did. Many current members of the BNP do look back on the Beackon episode as an embarrassment. There are a few intelligent people in positions of leadership. But we still need to subject the claim to critical scrutiny, and recent events tend to show that it is prejudice and stupidity which rule, as of old.

In May 2003 the BNP won five council seats in the Lancashire town of Burnley (though they did less well in June 2004). By 2004 they had 17 councillors in Britain. Membership had also grown: by that year they claimed to have 2,004 members. In Bradford 86 people joined in the first six months of 2004. However, the BNP has also lost members. One woman, Maureen Stowe, elected as a BNP councillor, resigned from the party and announced that she had never been a racist and felt she had been misled. At the time of writing she remains a councillor, but her public repudiation of the BNP seems to have had a significant impact. Of the BNP councillors who were elected, local observers have noted that their contribution to council discussions has been negligible. It may be that, like Beackon, they still do not understand what is going on, and lack the intellectual resources to contribute. Anti-racists, however, should not assume that, if this is the case now, it will always remain so. You don't have to be stupid to be a fascist, and it does help to co-opt some bright people. However, the record of fascist groups since Mosley has not been good in this area. Serious intellectuals have been conspicuous by their absence. Is it possible to build a political movement on the basis of lack of serious thought? The rise of Nazism suggests that the answer might be yes, provided that there is some ideological underpinning. But I guess that is not where we are in Britain with our tinpot little fascist groups. Nevertheless, caution and vigilance remain necessary.

At the time of writing, the BNP looks as if it might go the way of earlier fascist groups, the way of division, fragmentation and perhaps disintegration. Movements of this kind tend to attract people who want their own way and are often psychologically unstable; frequently their supporters do not fully understand the ideology of the group. They have a built-in tendency to split and split, and it may be that, after its worrying successes in some places, this will be the fate of the BNP too.

The importance of the presence of fascist and Nazi groups in encouraging racial conflict has been recognized by every reputable observer, not least by those commenting on recent events in Oldham, Burnley and elsewhere. When the 18-year-old black man Stephen Lawrence was murdered in Eltham in South London on 24 April 1993, informed observers noted the presence of the BNP head-quarters in nearby Welling as a factor in making racial violence respectable. Certainly in the south-east London area, reports of racial incidents had tripled in five years, with 811 recorded in 1992. Later in 1993, on 8 September, within days of the election of the first BNP councillor, Quddus Ali was beaten up in Commercial Road and suffered severe brain damage. There is no doubt that there is a link between the activity of racist and fascist organizations and the occurrence of violence. On the other hand, the BNP are quick to offer support to the white victims of black attacks, as they did after the murder of a white 15-year-old, Kriss Donald, in Pollokshields, Glasgow in March 2004.

Paki-bashing and beyond

In the East End of London, Brick Lane has played an important role in the history both of racial violence and of the response to it. Today, partly through the growth of 'Banglatown', the popular restaurant district pioneered by my friend Shirajul Hoque, and partly through the international success of Monica Ali's novel *Brick Lane*, the district has become famous as a cultural centre. In the 1970s it was rather different. The southern part of Brick Lane (in Whitechapel) had become the centre of the largest Bengali community in the world outside Bangladesh and the Indian subcontinent. But the northern part (in Bethnal Green) was a district historically associated with organized racism and fascism. This was the context of the violent events of the 1970s. Brick Lane became a danger zone, and skinhead violence aimed at the Bengali community was not uncommon.

At least 26 black people are known to have died between May 1976 and June 1981 as a result of racial violence in Britain. The Home Office report *Racial Attacks* in 1981 claimed that Asians were 50 times more likely than whites, and African-Caribbeans 36 times more likely, to be victims of racial attack. The study claimed that attacks were far more common than had been thought and were probably increasing. A study in Leeds in 1987 suggested that the actual incidence was probably ten times the official figures, while the New York based Human Rights Watch was later to claim that the official figure of 12,199 attacks between 1989 and 1996 was a serious underestimation. The figure for assaults between 1991 and 1994, they argued, was more likely to be around 32,000 per year. In 1993 Peter Lloyd, Minister of State at the Home Office, claimed, drawing on the British Crime Survey, that the true figure of racial incidents could be as high as 130–140,000 per year. In the same year the Commission for Racial Equality claimed that there were around 365 racial attacks each day.

Violence focused on Brick Lane itself reached a peak in 1978. After that year, it spread to outlying districts where Bengalis were fewer in number and less well organized. These years also showed either an increase in, or an increased recognition of, racially motivated incidents throughout the UK. Official figures from the Home Office showed an increase in the period 1988–92 from 4,383 to 7,734. Of the figure for 1992, 3,227 were in London alone. Metropolitan Police data showed a 22 per cent increase in racial incidents in 1989. The London Research Unit's housing survey in 1992 claimed that 48,000 households had experienced racist abuse or attacks. The number of attacks in London as a whole grew from 5,124 in 1993–4 to 5,480 in 1994–5.

On the Isle of Dogs 104 attacks were reported in 1987–8 although there were only 260 Bengali families living there. A report by Docklands Forum, *Racial Harassment in Docklands*, published in June 1990, showed that the majority of attacks in the area occurred in the Limehouse division, which included the Isle of Dogs. However, in the period before the election of the BNP councillor, the number of attacks increased markedly all over the East End. Between January 1993 and January 1994, attacks on the Isle of Dogs itself increased by 300 per cent, 71 per cent of victims being Asian. Assistant Commissioner Michael Taylor said that 'their presence is extremely likely to cause serious public disorder' *(Evening Standard,* 28 September 1993). In the East End, the figure grew to 643 in 1994, falling dramatically between 1995 and 1998, but increasing again to 8,898 in 1999.

In May 1989 the Home Office's Interdepartmental Racial Attacks Group produced a report entitled *The Response to Racial Attacks and Harassment: Guidance for the Statutory Agencies.* I had given evidence to this group, and the report was helpful. It stressed the importance of a multi-agency approach, although only seven out of its 138 pages dealt with this. The report did recognize that the problem was 'worryingly large' and that apparently trivial incidents were related to an 'insidious atmosphere'. It referred to what it called 'extremist organizations' which 'help to create a climate that is conducive to racial incidents' (p. 30). It claimed, wrongly, that 'the phenomenon of racial attacks and harassment has only begun to be uncovered in recent years' (p. 1), a strange admission of the government's ignorance of events that had been occurring over many years.

While this report was a sign of progress, it did expose the limitations of the statutory and bureaucratic approach. Without community action the recommendations of statutory groups would never have been made and will never have a major impact.

The situation today

When Derek Beackon was elected in Millwall in 1993, there was massive disillusionment with the Conservative government, the local Labour regime, and the 'Liberals' who had been ruling Tower Hamlets for some time. The neglected communities who lived in the shadow of Canary Wharf were angry – and rightly so. Support for the BNP was strongest among those who saw themselves as 'true islanders', for whom the neglect went back many decades. I heard one government minister describe this population as 'the latest layer of dust'. Contrary to David Blunkett, who, after the Bradford disturbances of 2001, saw fascism as a consequence of disorder, the historical evidence links it more with despondency and despair.

As the jubilant members of the BNP sang 'Rule Britannia' outside the Neighbourhood Offices on the night of 16 September 1993, a policeman confirmed the result had been declared. 'Yes, sir, the BNP *have held* this constituency' (my italics). His language showed how quickly the BNP had become part of the local political scene.

One aspect of the East London experience is the time lag between the rise of a racist movement and the consciousness of its significance among the people. The 'riots' in the summer of 2002 occurred in the old industrial towns, once the heart of the textile industry, and now largely deindustrialized. The response to these disturbances has been called 'community cohesion'.

Of course, groups such as the BNP are marginal and trivial compared with the Le Pen movement in France, neo-Nazi groups in Germany and Austria, or even pre-war British fascist movements of the Mosley type. The BNP membership is quite small. In 1993 it was estimated at 1,500–2,000, though some even then put it as low as 1,200. By 2002 the BNP themselves claimed a membership of 8,000, though others put the figure much lower, around 3,500. However, as statistics are unreliable, and individuals come and go, it is difficult to be sure. It is also unclear where the membership comes from. It seems not to be drawn from 'ordinary' members of the public but mainly from former members of the NF and other fascist groups. The membership seems to be mainly young, hence the nickname given to Beackon of 'Daddy Beackon' – though at the time of the 1993 election campaign he was only 49. (The term 'daddy' is common in prison usage.) One of the claims made by BNP spokesmen is that the thug element is inherited from NF days, though analysis of crime data in relation to age shows that this is incorrect. There is nothing new here either: fascist movements have always claimed that it is their opponents who are violent.

This is not to say that the BNP and similar groups are not highly dangerous, in terms of physical violence and, from time to time, the possibility of electoral success in certain localities. I would say, from long experience, that all the people I know who publicly attacked the fascist groups in the East End received death threats, obscene phone calls and abusive letters, and, more recently, some of them have appeared on the inflammatory Redwatch website. Most ordinary people who stay aside from opposition to these groups have little or no idea of what confronts those who do not. We are dealing with violent, in some cases severely mentally disturbed and deranged, people. (If you don't believe me, try attacking them in your local paper without withholding your address.)

Often racial violence occurs in areas where a particular community is a small minority, isolated and fearful. On the Manor estate in Sheffield, this was the situation of the fifty or so Somalis among a population of 6,000 white people several years ago. In periods of neglect and discontent, such groups can become an obvious target for attack.

It should be stressed too that international affairs have an effect on local incidents. Within two days of the attacks in the US on September 11, 2001, two Turks were attacked on the London Underground by thirty football supporters who tried to throw them down the escalators, while two days later an Afghan taxi driver was attacked with a bottle, beaten and left permanently paralysed. In the US, a Sikh gas station owner, Balbir Singh Sodhi, was shot and killed in the state of Arizona. The Associated Press reported that before shooting Sodhi, the murderer, Frank Silva Rogue, was reported to have said of the Middle Eastern population of the US, 'We should round them all up and kill them. We should kill their children, too, because they'll grow up to be like their parents.' This received a great deal of media coverage in the US.

It should also be recognized that an individual, infected with racist, fascist and related ideas, can quickly produce an acceleration of violence in a particular place. In April 1999, 22-year-old David Copeland was responsible for planting bombs that exploded in Brixton, South London (a major centre of the African-Caribbean community), in Brick Lane, East London (the heart of the

Bangladeshi community), and in Soho (a social centre for many gay people). I was in Brick Lane at the time of the second attack, and my flat was the last available place of refuge (and of lavatories!) before the police cordoned off the entire area.

What is the main role of the organized racist and fascist groups within local communities? I see it as threefold. First, these groups 'cash in on', and exploit, genuine grievances among the people, and translate them into crude racism, populism and hatred. Yet they seem to offer some hope and a sense of identity and purpose.

Second, they create, or accelerate, a climate of conflict and violence within areas which are already troubled.

Third, in this process they help to push the 'mainstream' parties in a more explicitly racist direction. This third element needs some elaboration.

We have seen in recent years how both Labour and Conservative politicians, worried by the appeal of racist and fascist groups, have felt that the best method of response is to go part of the way towards them. This is known in political history as appeasement, and it highlights a major danger for anti-racist work, not least by churches and religious groups. It is the danger that we focus on the 'extremist' groups and ignore the subtle ways in which their positions gradually seep into the rhetoric and practice of the mainstream parties. This is what, in 1978, I called 'creeping fascism'. The history of legislation on immigration is a classic example. The demands of 'Keep Britain White' groups were, over time, incorporated into government policy. The history is one of appeasement, compromise and collusion with prejudice, bigotry and hatred. Most of the positions on immigration, which were at one time espoused only by racist and fascist groups, gradually became normative in the Labour and Conservative parties – and governments.

Margaret Thatcher is an interesting, and almost classic, example of this phenomenon. To her the National Front consisted of 'twisted little men' with 'crackpot economics, jingoism and odious racialism'. However, she went on to stress, in a comment prior to the General Election of 1979, that 'it no longer matters what these revolting people say'. The Thatcher years saw the government undermine the racist groups by stealing many of their clothes.

At the local level, it is also worth mentioning that from time to time there arise middle class organizations which aim to appeal to such groups as white churchgoers, groups who are perceived as being threatened by an 'alien influx'. These organizations are more genteel, more polite and more bourgeois than the NF or the BNP, though their views may be similar. They tend to be led by 'men in grey suits' who can be plausible and even charming.

However, to lay the blame on extremist groups alone, ignoring the structural racism within the country as a whole, is never wise or correct. Oldham, Burnley, Dewsbury and other northern towns seem to be experiencing problems and events which other areas went through a long time ago. Some sharing of insights could be very helpful in preventing over-reaction, complacency or false panics. More important, it could encourage a more effective national mobilization against both the fascist groups and structural racism within British society. In the next chapter I want to consider how local communities have responded, and might respond in the future.

5 | Wrestling with the Monster: community action against racism

It is because tolerance is so timid that prejudice is so infectious.
(Ruth Glass (1989, p. 191))

Racism affects communities of different kinds, and does so in different ways, often appealing to and exploiting genuine local concerns. Racist ideology is often itself embodied in, and manifested through, organizations and groups which exist for the purpose of promoting or intensifying it. The members of these groups may have little idea of that underlying ideology except in the crudest way, as recent support for the British National Party shows. They may not read books and may have little or no understanding of history. But these racist political parties and paramilitary groups provide companionship, solidarity and an atmosphere in which racism can grow and prejudice can be reinforced. It is essential that anti-racists recognize the positive role of these groups. They often appeal to ordinary people in ways which the 'mainstream' parties do not. They exploit gut feelings of neglect and inability to 'get anything done'. They give people a sense of identity and involvement in political action, perhaps for the first time. It is particularly necessary to understand this appeal, and to take it seriously, at this historical moment when faith in 'mainstream' politics and parties is at such a low ebb, and when 'mainstream' politicians often seem very distant and remote.

Communities in particular geographical areas may find themselves attracted by racist explanations of their situation. The more I reflect on my own history in East London and elsewhere, the more important, it seems to me, is the need to try to change the climate which provides fertile ground for such explanations, and not simply attack racism in isolation. This is not a quick or simple thing to do. Of course, it has been, and still is, essential that protection is organized for the victims of racial violence, and that action is taken to prevent racist organizing. But it is more important, for the long term, to try to undermine those features within global, national and local societies that make racist explanations plausible, and therefore create a climate in which racial violence is likely. Sadly, political parties, churches and voluntary organizations often prefer to stay 'above the battle' and keep their heads down. Because of this aloofness from conflict, racist groups flourish. Aloofness from conflicts does not lead to their comprehension – or to their resolution.

As long ago as 1937 Wal Hannington, in his important book *The Problem of the Distressed Areas*, devoted a chapter to the question 'Is there a fascist danger among the unemployed?' While today's atmosphere is different, the question which Hannington raised is still relevant. Thousands of unemployed, ill-treated, neglected, badly housed people are open to the possibility of being taken in by racist or fascist accounts of their plight. My friendship with the East End Jewish Communists Phil Piratin and Solly Kaye helped me to see that it is essential to change the climate and the conditions, and not simply to attack racism. If such change does not occur, racist organizations may grow and achieve power, offering false answers to real grievances.

Sometimes, however, local communities rise up in protest against the presence of racism in their midst. Why they do this, or fail to do this, depends on a range of factors. Often a specific event, or series of events, provides the trigger for action. Again, it is vital that anti-racists are aware of what is happening, and are ready to respond to the event or the moment which could be the turning point in the struggle. In Christian terms, this is referred to as a *kairos* moment, a moment of critical importance and urgency which needs to be seized and acted upon, and which we neglect at our and everyone's peril. In this chapter I shall again draw on the experience in East London, looking at responses to racial violence in the 1970s, at the situation of the local community on the Isle of Dogs – confronted in 1993 by the election of the first BNP councillor in Britain – alluded to in Chapter 4, at more recent responses to the BNP and other racist groups in the last few years, and at the need for continuing vigilance.

For many years official responses to racial violence, by government and police, were marked by denial and complacency. It took a long time to force the issue on their attention, and by the time this had begun to happen, much damage had been done. So anti-racists are, to some extent, swimming against the tide, although there have been some signs of improvement since 1997. Many people who are now members of government in Britain were active in anti-racist work before they were elected. While this is no guarantee of anything, it is part of a history on which we need to build.

I want, first, to reflect on the events that occurred in the Brick Lane district of East London during the second half of the 1970s.

Responses to violence in Brick Lane

It is important, wherever we are, to identify locations where racial attacks are most prevalent, and to organize against them there. For example, during the time I spent in Chicago, of 1,122 'hate crimes' between 1992 and 1997, 207 occurred in parks. There were at that time 552 parks in Chicago, but over half of the attacks occurred in 23 of them. It was essential therefore to target those 23 parks. In East London in 1978, Bengalis and others identified quite precisely which districts were 'safe' and which were not (as Jewish groups had done in an earlier period). Racial attacks were concentrated in certain districts. On 17 July 1978, 8,000 Bengalis, including 300 schoolchildren, held a one-day strike in protest against racial attacks. In each area, it is really important to monitor the location of attacks, both to mobilize to prevent them, and to provide support for victims. A sense of the importance of geography is vital. (I often found in academic circles in London that the geographers understood what I was talking about better than the theologians!)

The raising of consciousness among the police was the result of a long struggle and is still uneven. It took a very long time to convince the police in East London both that racial violence was serious and also that the fascist groups were a threat to the common good. (Many police in the 1970s refused to accept that racial attacks existed at all, and a British Movement symbol remained on the wall of Bethnal Green Police Station for many weeks, the police claiming that they did not know what it was!) Police responses have never improved automatically as a result of goodwill or education among the police alone, but only as a result of pressure from outside.

People who criticize the police are often accused of being 'anti-police'. (In the same way, those who emphatically criticize the policies of the US are called 'anti-American'.) But criticism is vital if progress is to be made. I look back at my relations with the police in the 1970s with a mixture of horror, depression and amusement. Like many of my colleagues, and most of the victims of racial attacks, I eventually stopped phoning the police when an attack occurred. They never arrived until it was too late, if they arrived at all, and in many cases showed more interest in the immigration status of the victims than in tracing the attackers. On the day I left Bethnal Green, I was woken at 3 a.m. by two policemen who informed me that there was a 'naked light' in the church. They had just noticed in the upstairs window the light before the Blessed Sacrament which had been reserved there for a hundred years!

Ah! the police. Yet we cannot ignore them, and many of them are warm, committed and conscientious individuals. The problem has been the 'police subculture' which undoubtedly has reinforced racism along with sexism, a 'macho' ethos, stereotyping of groups and individuals (often within their own ranks), and (as a crucial component in the movement) alcoholism. It is difficult to be sure whether there has been much progress among the police in the area of action against racism. My impression is that there has, and that it is important both to encourage those who have worked for this, often against enormous resistance, and to remain critically vigilant because we are in the very early stages of change.

Responses from the statutory sector were also very uneven, and occurred slowly. The 1989 Home Office report, *The Response to Racial Attacks and Harassment,* included guidelines for the police and local authorities. But in East London we had endured twenty years of such attacks, and it was only after considerable pressure that the authorities took notice – and then, in the case of the police, claimed the credit for the belated action!

Most responses to racism are not made at the intellectual level. There are cultural aspects which must never be ignored. The Rock Against Racism movement, the brainchild of the Anti-Nazi League (ANL) and the Socialist Workers' Party (SWP) in the late 1970s, provides an interesting case study (Widgery, 1986). I was closely involved with two of the big events which fused the old-style political march with the carnival atmosphere characteristic of Notting Hill and of street festivals in smaller communities in other towns and cities. Just as the Jewish Communist joke in the 1930s claimed that the Mosley movement was defeated in the boxing ring as much as in street politics, so it could be claimed that rock music was a major factor in defeating racism and fascism in British cities. This can be grossly over-simplified and sentimentalized, but it is vital to recognize its significance as, for example, both Cornel West and Paul Gilroy have done in their writings.

Two incidents stick in my mind from the Carnival Against the Nazis in 1978. One was a moment when, as the 100,000 or so marchers turned from Commercial Street into Bethnal Green Road, we were jeered at by a hundred or so young NF supporters on the pavement chanting 'Sieg Heil! Sieg Heil!' At this moment the reggae group Steel Pulse abruptly stopped the music they were playing, and switched to 'Babylon Is Falling'. It was an incredibly powerful and deeply emotional moment. Joy, exuberance and exhilaration among the marchers met hatred and bitterness on the sidewalk. The contrast was electric. The second incident occurred the following day as I walked up Bethnal Green Road and met a group of white and mixed-race teenagers who I knew had been linked with the Young National Front. They were all proudly wearing Rock Against Racism badges. Of course, cynics would say they were simply following the fashion of the moment. The anti-racists had the best bands. But there is something deeper here which needs to be taken seriously. Anti-racism is not all in the head.

Rock Against Racism was revived in 1992, and now we have Love Music Hate Racism (LMHR) which, at the time of writing, has held over sixty events in 2003–4. We need to be wary of trying to recreate the past and use outdated methods that belong to a specific cultural period, but it is essential to learn from music and the visual arts, and to use the insights of musicians and other artists in community struggles.

A key figure in combating racism in East London has been my friend Dan Jones, for years secretary of the local Trades Council. Dan is an artist, and his paintings of events in East End history frequently appear in anti-racist publications and archives. Close to Dan's home in Cable Street a large mural on the wall of St George's Town Hall depicts the resistance to fascism in October 1936, an event which became known as 'the Battle of Cable Street'. Although Dan did not paint it, he was closely involved with the artists, and with many others whom he taught to paint. It is one example, among many, of the power of the visual arts to express community resistance to oppression.

Both Dan and I began our work in the East End with close links to the youth service and to 'detached youth work', and it is worth saying something about the role of youth workers in this field. In

1964, when I first became involved with the Hoxton Café Project, one of the earliest schemes set up to work with 'unattached youth', organized racism was building up again in adjacent neighbourhoods. A mile or two south was one of the oldest youth work projects in Britain, Avenues Unlimited, pioneered by Derek Cox who is still active in the area. In both cases anti-racist work was crucial, but it had to be done carefully, thoughtfully and on the basis of establishing trust, confidence and respect among the young people. This kind of slow work is not wasted time, and is crucial for the education of a coming generation.

The advantages of involving, or recognizing and valuing the involvement of, youth workers as critical agents in resistance to racism are many, but three seem to me important. First, youth workers are very close to vulnerable young people. They often live in the area, and are around at 'unsocial hours' when other 'professionals' (social workers, teachers, health workers) are not. Long-term residence in an area enables you to take 'the village' seriously, and to engage with its immediate as well as its long-term issues. Second, they belong to a tradition of work which has laid stress on human dignity and equality. And, third, they have access to educational resources which can be used in anti-racist work.

There are many examples of the role of youth workers in this field. Rewind in Sandwell in the West Midlands and the Manningham Project in Bradford come to mind, as well as Avenues Unlimited in East London. If we are to undermine what Phil Cohen terms the 'racist imagination', we will need to defend the youth service from attack and from the real danger of extinction.

The Isle of Dogs 1993–4

Accurate knowledge and 'intelligence' was, and is, very important in community action against racism. I have been associated since the 1960s with the anti-fascist magazine *Searchlight*, which began as a few duplicated sheets. Today it provides data, month by month, on racist and fascist organizations all over the world. It is vital reading for anyone involved in anti-racist work. But this needs to be complemented by intelligence work at the local level. So, in 1993 after the election in Millwall, we set up a BNP Monitoring Group, coordinated by Savi Hensman, Kaushika Amin and myself. As a result of increased fascist activity, especially in Poplar, the Isle of Dogs and

Bethnal Green, the group started to meet more frequently until the May 1998 local elections. Its purpose was to maintain an ongoing scrutiny of local fascist activity, and to liaise with other groups who were doing so. While we were aware of the limitations of simply giving information, the initiative of Docklands Forum in publishing the report, written by Caroline Adams and Gilli Salvat, *Once Upon a Time in Docklands: facts and figures in the 1990s*, in 1994 was an important contribution to the defeat of the BNP. We had realized that much opposition to racist groups was very woolly, vague and lacking in accurate knowledge. So the stress on accurate information is very important. Yet purely rational arguments are not likely to be effective among those who are not very rational, have deep feelings of alienation and disappointment, and will not respond at an intellectual level. Action for justice in the areas where it affects them is more likely to undermine racial conflict.

It was even more important to realize that many people voted for the BNP out of sheer despair, frustration, anger and disillusionment, and should not be written off as irredeemable racists. The vote for the BNP was described by the Jewish historian David Cesarani as 'more an assertion of community spirit than a protest against immigration'. Anyone who has been involved with local 'community politics', rooted in a love and affection for one's home territory, can, under certain circumstances, be twisted in a racist direction. This happened to some extent on the Isle of Dogs in 1993, as it had happened in the aftermath of Saul Alinsky's community organizing in the 'back of the yards' meat packing district of Chicago forty years earlier. One of the key questions we always need to ask when the word 'community' is used is: Who is being excluded here?

One fact which emerged in the Isle of Dogs, and has generally done so in Britain, has been the lack of contact between communities. As we have seen, a study in July 2004 suggested that 90 per cent of white people had no black friends, although the position was improving in the younger age groups. Of course, contact is only one aspect of overcoming racism, but it should not be ignored. In fact it is a major problem in many areas of social action. For all their moral commitment, many campaigners against poverty seem to have very little, if any, regular personal contact with poor people.

Responses to attacks have in some cases brought out the basic decency and goodness of individuals. When Mukhtar Ahmed, aged

18, was beaten up in Bethnal Green, for instance, it was the girl-friend of one of the attackers, appalled by his boasting about the attack, who informed the police. When Kriss Donald was killed in Pollokshields in March 2004, his mother commented that the killers were 'five men driven by hate' and that their colour did not matter.

The BNP in Millwall were defeated by a well-organized coalition of the churches, trade unions and local Bengali groups, involving much laborious activity of a humdrum and undramatic kind. The BNP vote still increased at the next election in May 1994. They were defeated because vastly more people voted, and this was to happen later in another local ward. In December 1994 the BNP again got 20 per cent of the vote in the local elections. Increasing the overall vote was crucial, though it was only one aspect of changing the social and political climate.

As in the earlier success – though not in electoral terms – of the National Front in Bethnal Green and Shoreditch in the 1970s, what defeated the fascists was the commitment of local activists to work with and for all sections of the community, to combat racism in the context of class and wider dimensions of oppression, and the visible evidence that the fascists had neither the will, the moral calibre nor the intelligence to do any of these things.

Recent responses to the BNP and other racist groups

The recent successes of the BNP are worrying but not surprising. They have built on the perceived lack of concern for working class people in deprived communities. If they have the effect of awakening the 'mainstream' parties to this reality, they will have done something useful. Alienation of people from politics is a very serious matter, and it creates a vacuum which racist and fascist groups will quickly occupy.

One problem is that many mainstream politicians, middle class and well educated, tend to operate on a view of 'rationality' that is very intellectual and individualistic. But this is not how the mass of the people work. Opinions are formed, not as a result of 'reading the evidence' (as if that were neutral anyway), but in terms of a fusion of emotion, intellect and observation of immediately perceived local realities. No amount of argument at the intellectual level alone will shift people away from a racist explanation of their plight: there has to be a shift in the ground on which they stand. This was something which Phil Piratin, the Jewish Communist MP for Mile End in East London in the late 1940s, realized.

Let me therefore list ten dangers which need to be avoided. They are not the only ones, but, in my experience, they constantly reappear.

i   The danger of focusing too much on racist groups. Important as it is to combat these groups, it is easy to give them a great deal of attention – and publicity which may encourage them in some situations – at the cost of ignoring the diffused racist attitudes and practices in the general population.

ii   The danger of substituting demonstrations and public meetings for necessary slow, ongoing, boring, undramatic activity. Demonstrations and meetings are also important, but there is much more to be done.

iii The danger of ignoring examples of racism which are not so well publicized. If we are to avoid this, it is essential to monitor local situations carefully and not to rely simply on the media.

iv   The danger of locating the opposition wrongly, and so engaging in dialogue when confrontation is needed, or the opposite danger of being so confrontational in every situation that prejudices and positions are reinforced, not changed. Deciding which situations call for patient discussion, and which call for firm non-cooperation, resistance and implacable opposition requires thoughtful discernment.

v   The danger of playing down the physical threat presented by racist groups. These are not ordinary political parties. Many of their members have convictions for violent criminal activity, and people need to be aware of this. This emphatically does not mean giving in to intimidation, but it does mean realizing the dangers and taking them on board in all planned activities.

vi   The danger of ignoring wider issues such as housing, employment and education. Racism is indivisible. We cannot attack it in one place and collude with it in others.

vii The danger of ignoring 'mainstream' and 'genteel' forms of racism in social institutions such as churches, hospitals and universities. In some ways the NF and the BNP, in their crudeness and obnoxiousness, may be easier to cope with than their more genteel counterparts.

viii The danger of responding too quickly, without thought, and therefore sometimes making a situation worse. Anti-racist groups need to think as well as act.

ix The danger of elitism, sectarianism and narrowness of perspective. This often involves assuming that we 'know it all', and so failing to learn from our mistakes, or failing to recognize new situations that demand new responses.

x The danger of becoming exhausted, with the result that the struggle against racist groups is weakened. Taking care of oneself is a moral duty for all anti-racists. As the poet Denise Levertov once wrote, the common struggle suffers if those who work for it are 'hollowed out self neglectors'.

Let me expand on some of the above points. Local authority lethargy, inaction or discrimination can give ammunition and encouragement to racist groups. Take, for example, the case of Oldham in Lancashire, northwest England, where, in 2002, the ethnic minority population was 13 per cent, but ethnic minority representation in the council staff was only 2.6 per cent. Since then there have been significant improvements, many of them due to the work of anti-racist groups and individuals, some due to well-publicized 'riots'.

It is vital not to operate in a narrow and sectarian way but to draw in a wide range of groups. The role of schools, churches, mosques and 'community projects' is important. However, it is easy for 'anti-racism' to be seen as a series of middle class directives which may be obeyed but are not internalized.

It is important to take seriously the rise of the racist and fascist groups but, on the other hand, not to exaggerate their importance. There are both parallels and striking contrasts between the success of the Front National in France, and the reappearance of fascist and 'fascistoid' parties elsewhere in Europe, and the situation of the 'far right' in Britain. (I use the German term 'fascistoid' to indicate groups which are strongly influenced by classical fascism, but which do not conform to all the features of the earlier tradition.) There are close parallels in terms of ideology. Fascist and racist networks are well organized, feed off each other, and share common ideas – Holocaust denial, racial purity myths, and so on. Anti-racists need to recognize that, while some of these groups from time to time claim to have abandoned their racist and antisemitic past, this is usually not the case, and we should never take their claims at face value.

One aspect of the appeal of groups of the NF/BNP type is the crucial importance of areas adjacent to, yet separated from and often ignorant of, those, perhaps very close, with significant ethnic minority populations. As we have seen, in the 1930s the success of the BUF in the East End lay in the almost entirely white 'villages' of Shoreditch and Bethnal Green rather than in the more racially mixed areas to the north and south of them. As long ago as the census of 1881, Bethnal Green represented, in the words of researcher Charles Booth, the 'absolute low water mark' for immigration. Over a century later, the journalist Ruth Picardie, reporting the funeral of Bethnal Green gangster Ronnie Kray, described it as 'a celebration of the lost might of the white working class' (*Independent*, 9 May 1995). The former NF leader, Martin Webster, forcecasting success at a by-election in Rotherham in 1976, grasped the point:

> We shall do well in Rotherham. The presence of a strong immigrant population is not the vital factor. The Front does best when an immigrant problem is in sight nearby. We find that creates the better prospect.

Today many of the areas which support the BNP are areas with few black people and few immigrants but much fear and anxiety.

Although it is not always the case, it is important to remember that many racist activists seem very stupid. Derek Beackon, the first elected BNP councillor, must still be an embarrassment to that party. He once claimed that a local housing estate in East London, Masthouse Terrace, was almost entirely Asian, and a 'no go area' for whites. When told that the Asian population was 28 per cent, he replied that this was more than half! Of course, we cannot rely on such levels of ignorance being sustained, but it is important also not to assume that one's racist opponents are intelligent. The history suggests otherwise. Purely intellectual methods therefore are not likely to be effective.

The use of the local media is important. On the day of the election on 23 September 1993, the *East London Advertiser* ran a front page headline, 'Would *you* vote for the BNP?' There is evidence that this headline and article helped to defeat the BNP. But it did not happen without effort. It was the result of careful attention to the role of the press, and action based on this.

It is often said that, in its recent manifestations and successes, the BNP has become more 'sophisticated'. There is some truth in this.

The desire to appear respectable, and worthy of support by middle Britain, has been a feature of some members of far right groups since the founding of the NF in 1967. It has also been a cause of division within these groups. Today the BNP does concentrate on, and has some success in, comfortable suburban and rural communities as well as deprived urban ones. My suspicion, however, is that we need to look for 'sophisticated' or 'genteel' forms of racism more in the mainstream parties. It is possible that the BNP in the future may attract not so much the 'respectable' as the deranged, violent, and psychopathic elements in society.

However, while the appeal of these groups is increasingly to diverse sections of the community – poor people and middle class people, inner city and suburban residents, and so on – we should not ignore their continued attraction to what is often called the 'underclass' of despondent white youth. It was Martin Webster again who, in 1979, claimed that 'the social base of the National Front is made up of the desperate and the dispossessed among the white working class'. It is vital that Christians and others who are opposed to racism and fascism do not, as they have done frequently in the past, ignore this group or write them off as beyond the pale. This was a point made by the MacDonald inquiry of January 1990 into the murder of Ahmed Iqbal Ullah in Manchester. The report drew attention to the failure to help white students, and attacked what it called 'moral and symbolic anti-racism'.

In some sections of the population, racial prejudice has for many years been viewed as a psychological disturbance, and one wing of anti-racism has moved into a kind of therapeutic style with a stress on 'consciousness training' and 'race awareness'. However, the story is complex and confusing. Traditional psycho-analysis has, as I pointed out earlier, been almost silent on the question, although Reich (1945) emphasized the fear of sex and the concern with purity, while Adorno (1950) drew attention to aggression and the need to protect the personality from dissolu-tion. We need to be careful, however, not to view racism purely in terms of personal pathology. Certainly many members of racist and fascist groups are people with serious mental health problems. Tom Linehan's study of East London support for Oswald Mosley in the 1930s revealed within the pro-Mosley groups a recurring sense of pessimism and a dread of decay, dissolution and the collapse of the old familiar world. Helping people to cope with upheaval and change and to see alternatives to a fascist response is of critical importance.

From my own experience I would want to emphasize the need for small scale, local and provisional action, linked with the readiness to realize that, as the nature of racist organizing changes, so must the responses; and with the importance of locating racism within the wider framework of injustice and oppression outside which it is incomprehensible and apart from which it cannot be resisted and defeated.

It is essential that those involved in anti-racist work have credibility, and this takes time. We need to have, or to establish, roots within the local area. We need to be respected, trusted, taken seriously, even when people disagree with us. In the East End, individuals such as the teacher and social worker Edith Ramsey, the Jewish Communist Solly Kaye, Fr John Groser, the Bengali leader Tassaduq Ahmed, and many others, were heard because they had established a reputation for solid, reliable and consistent work for justice for all the people. There is no substitute for this, but it involves long-term commitment.

There are many lessons for Christians here, but three are particularly urgent. First, we cannot ignore the appeal of fascism to, and its historical roots within, parts of the Christian tradition, Catholic and Protestant, as in the overwhelming support for Franco among Roman Catholics or the feeling, among some leading Anglican bishops, that Hitler was both a force for moral reform and a bulwark against Communism.

Second, churches cannot stay 'above the battle', uttering vague moral appeals in a disconnected way. We will only be taken seriously if we are seen to be committed in the detail, and that will always involve pain, conflict and violence.

Third, the conflict with fascism and racism lies at the very heart of the gospel and of the nature of the Church. It is not an optional extra, not a specialized activity for certain boards, committees and working parties. It is far more fundamental than most of the issues that modern Christians get worked up about. I will say more about this in Chapter 6.

6 | Putting on Christ: race and the Christian community

Many groups admitted that very little had been done under this priority. Some found it difficult to identify the problem, and so there was little perception that anything needed to be done.

(Roman Catholic Diocese of Westminster's East London Area Responses to the Area Pastoral Assembly reporting on racism, 22 February 1981)

Christianity is not primarily a philosophy but a crusade. As Christ was sent by the Father, so he sends his disciples to set up in the world the Kingdom of God . . . He was manifested to destroy the works of the devil. Hence when Christians find in the world a state of things which is not in accord with the truths which they have learned from Christ, their concern is not that it should be explained but that it should be ended.

(J. H. Oldham (1925, p. 26))

He [Christ] . . . has broken down the dividing wall, that is, the hostility between us . . . So he came and proclaimed peace to you who were far off and peace to those who were near.

(Ephesians 2.14, 17)

Some years ago a well-meaning white liberal English bishop wrote a letter to churchwardens in each parish in his diocese about the importance of making ethnic minorities welcome in the churches. The letter had taken account of recent debates within the Church about racial justice, and it contained all the right sentiments. It had only one fatal flaw. It was quite obvious from the way in which the letter was written that he took for granted that all the individuals to whom he was writing were white. In fact, a good number of the wardens, and many members – in some areas the majority – of the congregations were black. It was a classic example of the assumed leadership of the dominant white community, a community which has often taken its role for granted. I shall suggest later that the whole edifice of 'whiteness', with its history of domination, needs to be confronted and set free from its constructed and sustained invisibility.

The black Christian tradition

Most Christians today are black, or at least not of Anglo-Saxon origin. (It is perhaps even worth reminding white readers that the Christian movement itself began in the Middle East, only spreading to 'white' areas later.) This is true not only within urban areas of the UK – 50 per cent of churchgoers in London are black, for example – but globally. The typical Anglican in the world is probably a young black woman in Africa. When we look beyond Anglicanism, which is, after all, a minority tradition among Christian movements, black Christianity is an enormous, powerful and growing force through-out the world (as indeed is Hispanic Christianity, both in Central and South America and the US). It is valuable to begin with the black Christian tradition, not simply because it is historically extremely important, but also because, as a matter of statistical fact, a high proportion – if not the majority – of practising Christians globally are black. White Christians in the UK tend to forget this if they ever knew it, although the fantastic growth of the black-led churches within the UK itself may even have helped to change their minds.

But it is not just a matter of changing minds. A change in per-sonal and social consciousness, in orientation, in perspective is needed, and for white Christians this must surely mean liberation from the tyranny and captivity of 'whiteness'. By this I do not, of course, mean the abandonment of the fact that many Christians are 'white', or, more accurately, pinko-grey, in their physical complex-ion. I do mean the abandonment of the myth that 'whiteness' is normative, dominant, central to Christian reality. Yet this process of abandonment is not simple, for the structures of domination within the world's major churches are inextricably bound up with 'white-ness'. The Roman communion is dominated politically by white male Italians, and culturally by the Irish – though the odd Pole manages to intrude, and survive for a long time to be replaced by a German! Anglicanism is still dominated by Canterbury, a city in the very white English county of Kent. Eastern Orthodoxy is overwhelmingly organized from within the Greek, Slavic and Russian communities (although the Ethiopian Orthodox have attracted many black Christians with no geographical link to North Africa). So most Christians are black – what does this mean in terms of global politics, and of Christian praxis? The issue is a complex one, but it cannot be evaded.

The allegiance of black people to Christianity is rooted in specific histories. In the US, for example, many slaves became Baptist, and the Baptist churches are still a major force within American black Christianity. They represent a major public sphere for survival and for the nourishing of alternative vision. This is significant and worth noting, not least because the Southern Baptist church (one of many politically and socially diverse 'Baptist' churches in America) is a reactionary political group in the US, was a major bulwark in electing President Bush and, with some exceptions, is deeply racist. Yet black Christians have found in the Baptist tradition a source of resistance, manifested most powerfully in recent decades in the witness of Martin Luther King, Jr.

Other black Christians are identified with the Pentecostal tradition, which grew from the Holiness movements of the late nineteenth century and from the Azusa Street revival in Los Angeles in the early twentieth century. Cornel West in the US and Robert Beckford in the UK, who both belong to this tradition, are among a number of recent black Christian theologians who have stressed the need for a prophetic voice from within the black churches. In recent years, in both the US and the UK, urban black-led churches have played a greater role in economic development and in community action. (Those churches where there is direct influence from Africa will be aware that a key word in Swahili is *ujamaa*, cooperative economics.)

In Britain, the Aladura churches, Christ Apostolic, and the Cherubim and Seraphim flourish among Nigerian Christians. There are other African churches, and churches of African-Caribbean origin, as well as those which grew out of the US and spread via Jamaica to Britain. (On the Jamaican background see Austin-Broos, 1997.) Of the latter, the most significant are the New Testament Church of God and the Church of God of Prophecy, both of which have a large presence in inner city areas of England. Originating in Tennessee, the Church of God and its offshoots are, in the US, mainly white and rural: only in Jamaica and England are they mainly black and urban. Theologically, these churches grew out of the Southern plantocracy and inherited the pietistic theology of revivalism. It is this otherworldly theology which is now being called into question within the British context.

Jawanza Kunjufu has divided black-led churches into three groups: entertainment churches ('sing, shout and holler'); containment churches, essentially churches of the status quo; and liberation churches which seek transformation. White Christians may find nothing new here, for the same divisions exist in the white-led churches. However, it is important to pay attention to what is happening within some of the black-led churches. Many observers, black and white, write off the black Pentecostal churches as hopelessly apolitical and otherworldly. Certainly, as Robert Beckford has said, 'many black Pentecostals are simply unaware of the socio-political motivations that produced their Christian tradition' (Beckford, 2001, p. 5). But a process of radicalization and deeper prophetic understanding about the wholeness of the gospel message has been taking place, much of it influenced by black Christians such as Cornel West, James Cone, Desmond Tutu, Patrick Kalilombe, Robert Beckford, Jacquelyn Grant, Katie Cannon and many others. Alongside this has been a grass roots movement which has led many black Christians in the inner cities of Britain to reject as unbiblical and wrong the 'otherworldliness' of the white revivalist traditions which gave them birth. Black Christian thinkers in Britain such as Io Smith, Joel Edwards, Robert Beckford and Ron Nathan have been important in aiding and influencing this shift, while in the Church of England the testimony of John Sentamu, Rose Hudson-Wilkin, Eve Pitts, Lorraine Dixon, Eileen Lake and others has been crucial. But it would be wrong simply to list well-known names. The black-led churches, and black Christian communities in all the UK churches, are changing dramatically, and we will see in the coming years a real grass roots ecumenism which will be evangelical, Pentecostal, deeply worship-centred, but also incarnational, redemptive and political in its resistance to injustice and oppression.

New critical voices are continually appearing within the black communities, calling much conventional ministry to account. A black student in the University of London has written: 'Some of the vicars go into the streets of Brixton to preach, but the youth are not interested. Have they got a message that is attractive to the youth? I think not' (Nathan, 1998, p. 22).

Yet, as Bob Dylan memorably sang, 'the times they are a changin'', and we are in the midst of powerful transformations in the field of responses to racism and in the Christian witness to the righteousness of God.

This resurgence of black Christianity is, of course, a global phenomenon. But my sense is that to call it the 'next Christendom', as Philip Jenkins does, is a serious oversimplification, indeed a distortion of what is taking place. Rather than invoke the old language of Christendom, it is probably better to speak of a 'new Pentecost'.

The legacy and response of white Christianity

Yet while today the majority of practising Christians are black, or originate in the 'Third World', we cannot forget the fact that modern racism owes much of its ideological apparatus to Christianity, or rather to the 'infected Christianity' which passes for Christian orthodoxy. The term 'infected Christianity' seems first to have been used by George Mosse in his 1978 book *Towards the Final Solution*, and was further developed by Alan Davies (1988). It refers to a distortion, a virus, a development within Christianity which has made it open to racist influence. It was the Calvinist Diaspora which sowed the seeds of theological racism – a fact strangely missing from R. H. Tawney's classic study *Religion and the Rise of Capitalism* – while both the Eastern Orthodox and Roman traditions have reinforced ethnic forms of Christian presence. Anglicanism has promoted a white, often middle class and refined type of 'Englishness' around the world with all the peculiar consequences which we are now seeing as they emerge from places which earlier missionaries might have thought unlikely. It could be argued that much of this white exported Christianity has played a key role in the shaping of modern racism. Indeed Kyle Hazelden, writing from the North American context, argued that this kind of Christianity did more harm than atheism in the field of race relations (Hazelden, 1966, p. 17).

'There was little perception that anything needed to be done.' This depressing conclusion of the Roman Catholic Diocese of Westminster's East London Area Reponses to the Area Pastoral Assembly on 22 February 1981 was not untypical of the British churches as a whole, though this was a time when the raising of consciousness began, and action was first initiated. To understand this, it is essential to go back to the arrival of significant numbers of black Christians from the Caribbean and elsewhere in the years after the Second World War. At the time of migration from the Caribbean it is estimated that around 90 per cent of practising Christians there belonged to five 'mainstream' churches – Roman Catholic, Anglican, Methodist, Baptist and Moravian – and less than 10 per cent to all the other religious groups put together. The British churches, and the Church of England in particular, were therefore in a strong position to relate to the newcomers, not least because Anglicanism, particularly in Barbados, had become an integral element within sections of the Caribbean working class to a greater degree than it had among the white working class in English cities. It is probably true to say that the churches were also in a strong position to mobilize opposition to discriminatory legislation. Yet a commitment to equality and justice, both at the pastoral and at the institutional level, not to mention a willingness to risk conflict with the government, was missing. The story of the failure of churches to engage with their new members on a basis of equality is a tragic one, well documented by Renate and John Wilkinson and others. Their failure to engage politically with the issues within a class-divided society, a society which black immigrants were entering, was part of a more complex history.

Of course, there were exceptions – some churches which took black people seriously, some church leaders who were active in the anti-racist struggle at an early stage, and so on – but the bulk of church work in relation to black immigrants can best be summed up as one of chaplaincy. There were a number of 'chaplaincies to coloured people', and the main focus was on race relations as an aspect of personal relations. The approach was idealist, the language that of harmony and reconciliation rather than justice and equality, and there was little sense that anything needed to change other than the individual heart. Much of the literature from church sources was simplistic, often bordering on the sentimental. Clifford Hill's popular 1958 book *Black and White in Harmony* was typical. Its cover showed a black child and a white child seated at a piano, playing both black and white notes: it was a picture that figured frequently in church discussions in these years.

Three features were conspicuously absent from church concerns in this period. First, there was no sustained critique of the campaign for immigration controls, while the Act of 1962 was generally accepted. Indeed, as far as the hierarchy was concerned, race did not seem to figure as an issue at all. The Archbishop of Canterbury throughout the 1950s, Geoffrey Fisher, was concerned about artificial insemination, premium bonds and homosexuality, but not apparently about race, and even the Lambeth Conference of 1958 took the view that racial discrimination was not widespread in Britain. A review of comments on race by bishops in 1955 showed that dominant themes were the absence of any colour bar, the danger of 'Little Harlems' in Britain, and the wrongness of 'mixed' marriages.

Second, there was no recognition of the place of colonialism in shaping church life itself. The failure to welcome, and in some cases the explicit rejection of, black people by the Anglican and other churches has been a significant factor in the massive growth of the black-led Pentecostal and Adventist churches. As mass religious movements among urban blacks in Britain, they are a post-immigration, post-racist phenomenon. Having their origins in American fundamentalist missions to the Caribbean, these churches had a theology which was otherworldly, escapist and pietist, rooted in the racially segregated world of Tennessee and other southern states, and ill-equipped (and unwilling) to engage with racism, either theologically or politically. Only in recent years has this begun to change.

Third, there was no recognition of the way in which racism exposed other forms of oppression and injustice within the structures of the church. Engagement with these issues was slow to develop, and by the time it began, a generation of black Christians had been lost to the 'mainstream' churches. As Michael Ramsey, Archbishop of Canterbury, said in the House of Lords on 12 March 1962, the church was 'woefully behind' on the issue of race.

I have shown in earlier pages that towards the end of the 1960s the older use of the word 'racism' gave way to its employment with structural, systemic and institutional connotations. The word was reintroduced to English usage to refer to institutional racism, racism systematically reproduced through an organization's or a society's ostensibly a-racist practices. (It is an indicator of how slow organizations and media have been to understand this concept that the term 'institutional racism' is still being debated, in the aftermath of the MacPherson report on the Stephen Lawrence murder, as if it were a new idea.) The shift in usage can be traced fairly precisely to 1969, and to the thinking which led to the establishment of the World Council of Churches' Programme to Combat Racism in August of that year. Earlier, at its assembly in Uppsala in 1968, the Council had defined racism in terms of pride and doctrine, but the Consultation on Racism, held in Notting Hill in May 1969, moved beyond this, using the term 'institutional racism' and emphasizing structural dimensions. It is clear that the Notting Hill Consultation marked a turning point in the thinking of many Christians. The Consultation established that racist ideologies were tools in economic, political and military struggles for power, and that, once developed, they had a life of their own. It called the churches to account, insisting 'that they no longer concentrate their attention on improving race relations at an individual level but on striving for racial justice and a new balance of power at the level of institutions'.

The ripples of Notting Hill quickly spread around the Christian world. In August 1969 the Central Committee of the World Council of Churches became one of the first bodies to use the term 'institutional racism':

It is no longer sufficient to deal with the race problem at the level of person to person relationships. It is institutional racism as reflected in the economic and political power structures which must be challenged. Combating racism must entail a redistribution of social, economic and cultural power from the powerful to the powerless.

Nevertheless, it took many years for the churches in Britain to take racism with any kind of practical seriousness. In the early 1970s the Advisory Council for the Church's Ministry produced a textbook on *Teaching Christian Ethics* for use in theological colleges. The final draft dealt with the whole area of race in eight lines which included, as its only item of recommended reading, Anthony Richmond's Penguin *The Colour Problem*, published in 1955! While the published version contained some minor changes, mainly in the bibliography, it included no attention to racism as such. This was the main academic text used in teaching ethics to those preparing for ordained ministry at this time.

A turning point among Methodists was Heather Walton's report *A Tree God Planted*, published by the Ethnic Minorities Working Party in 1985. Prior to the end of the 1960s the perception of what was termed 'the race problem' in the church consisted of two elements. First, there was a recognition of the reality of prejudice, discrimination and spasmodic racial violence, but these phenomena were seen as regrettable aberrations, blots on the landscape, deviations from the British way of life. All that was needed to remove or reduce them was a strong dose of goodwill and purity of heart. 'Race relations' was seen as one aspect of personal relations. Second, there was a recognition that some insidious groups were active who held a doctrine of racial superiority, but they were not seen as significant. Indeed, to draw attention to them was seen as likely to encourage them. This probably remained the dominant perception for some ten years after the founding of the National Front in 1967.

It was the coming of Margaret Thatcher, and the growth of the 'radical right', of the social authoritarian tendency, and of a new mutation of racism within the Conservative Party, that forced the churches on to the offensive in relation to issues of justice generally, and ironically led to a renewal of Christian social and political critique. However, immediately prior to the Thatcher victory, there had been an important debate within the churches on Gus John's pamphlet *The New Black Presence in Britain*. The session devoted to this document in the General Synod on 6 July 1977 was the key discussion which prepared the way for later developments. The churches' increased engagement in the Thatcher period with poverty and deprivation, their response to the 1981 urban uprisings, the appointment of a Race Relations Field Officer for the Church of England, the General Synod's support for the Race Relations Projects Fund of the (then) British Council of Churches, the publication of *Faith in the City*, local churches' concrete struggles over asylum, deportation and sanctuary, the growth of the Churches' Commission for Racial Justice and numerous similar groups within the different denominations – all these helped to raise the profile, and the seriousness, of the churches' increased concern with racial justice. By 1985 the Secretary of the Joint Council for the Welfare of Immigrants could say that the Church of England was the 'only established institution which has consistently angered the present government and its supporters with its stand on race and immigration issues', while a headline in the *Church Times* ten years later, announcing 'Churches "in forefront" of anti-racism fight' reflected a major shift in consciousness and praxis.

It is arguable that the Church found it easier to respond to issues of racism in 'society', and that there was less perception of the same issues within the Church itself. When a working party of the Church of England's Board for Social Responsibility recommended disinvestment from South Africa, the members had their travel expenses paid on Barclays Bank cheques, though Barclays, the bankers to the Central Board of Finance of the Church of England, were widely seen as 'bankers to apartheid'. As late as 1986, Church House, the national headquarters of the Church of England in Westminster, followed the policies of the civil service in everything from entry passes to salary scales – except equal opportunities policy and ethnic monitoring!

Not surprisingly, the areas in which least progress has been made in the 'mainstream' churches have been those of class and power. The relationship of the churches to working class and poor people is complex. In some areas there is evidence that the churches are engaged with and working with what is increasingly termed the 'underclass' to a greater degree than other organizations, and Cornel West has claimed that Christianity is 'a religion specially fitted to the oppressed'. That is not by any means the whole story, but it is part of the story, however much the secular left may find it embarrassing and inconvenient. Of course ultimately the issue of power is paramount. Marx pointed out that the Church of England would sooner give up thirty-eight of its thirty-nine articles than one thirty-ninth of its income. Today, more and more church members realize the centrality of a commitment to economic and political change, and see this as a theological task.

Theology and racism

Throughout my engagement with the churches around issues of racism from the 1960s to the 1980s, one fact was quite startling. While there was much pastoral work of a compassionate and justice-oriented kind, it seemed that racism was never perceived as a threat to the heart of the gospel, a rejection of the baptismal covenant, a denial of the Christian faith. My view is that the Church will never make progress in this area until we see opposition to racism as being central to biblical faith, incorporated at the heart of its liturgy and life, repeated regularly in credal commitment. This must involve regular and serious theological preaching, as well as discussion, good collects, hymns, songs, pictures and so on, and spiritual direction which will help to shape the character of the Christian person. It must involve taking seriously the fact that racism distorts and damages the life of the spirit. For racism is not simply a mistaken political option: it is, as Nikolai Berdyaev saw in 1935, 'a crude materialism which has taken a mystical character' and become a substitute for true spirituality (Berdyaev, 1935, p. 98). It is in fact an alternative gospel.

So, on the four central questions of the nature of humanity, the potential for human love, the nature and scope of grace, and the character and purpose of the Church itself, racism is in conflict with orthodox Christian faith. Take, first, the nature of humanity. In racist thought, the nation takes precedence over the human race. Loyalty, devotion and responsibility can only be to the nation, not to humanity as a whole. The state of nationhood becomes the normal human state. But the sense of unity as a nation is, on this view, only possible where people are of common racial stock. So the Northern Irish and the Falkland Islanders are part of the British nation in a way that British-born black people can never be. The fascist leader John Tyndall once said that the fatal flaw in Christianity was its belief that love could extend beyond the bounds of race and nation.

Throughout racist rhetoric the theme of 'human nature' constantly occurs. Thus Enoch Powell, speaking in Eastbourne on 16 November 1968, described the English as being 'dislodged' from their homeland. However, he argued, 'the people of England will not endure it . . . I do not believe that it is in human nature that a country . . . should passively watch the transformation of whole areas which lie at the heart of it into alien territory.' In later speeches Powell spoke of 'operating with human nature as it is' rather than seeking to alter it. Other MPs spoke of preference for one's own race as being, in Ivor Stanbrook's words on 5 July 1976, 'simply human nature'.

This kind of language is in clear opposition to the Jewish and Christian scriptures, where the only race referred to is the human race, *ho genos ton anthropon*. Human beings are the offspring of God, *tou gar kai genos semen* (Acts 17.28). The Eastern Orthodox tradition stresses that human solidarity in and with God is not a supernatural gift but the very core of human nature, while in the west Julian of Norwich insisted that 'our nature . . . is joined to God in its creation'. It is this human nature that Christ shared and took into the life of God. Human nature is thus fundamentally open to God and to the workings of God's grace: it is not static and unchanging, irredeemably tribal and narrow. It is open to change and transformation. The claim that 'You can't change human nature' is so fundamentally anti-Christian that, if taken seriously, it would undermine the whole of Christian faith. In racist understanding, what matters most about the human person is her or his ethnic or 'racial' origin; to the Christian, what matters is that she or he is made in God's image and shines with the divine light. Christians also believe that, through his life, death and resurrection, Jesus united humanity to God in an even closer and more fundamental way. This is what we call the Incarnation, the en-fleshing of the divine Word and the taking of humanity into God. The late Eric Mascall saw the working out of the consequences of this incarnational faith as being central to the theology of the future:

> Human existence and human history can never be the same again since the moment when God the Son united human nature to himself in a union which will never be dissolved. It will be one of the tasks of the theology of the future to work out the implications of this amazing truth, for, apart from occasional adumbrations in such fathers as St Irenaeus, the theology of the past, especially in the west, has paid little attention to it. (Mascall, 1968, p. 133)

I believe that one of the implications of which Mascall spoke is the incompatibility of any form of racist ideology and practice with incarnational Christian faith.

John Davies, writing from the experience of many years in South Africa, stresses the centrality of the visible Body of Christ, the community which derives from the Incarnation:

> The most powerful weapon in Catholicism's armoury of imagery in the struggle against injustice is the doctrine of the Body of Christ . . . There has been nothing radical or intellectually daring about this: the South African situation has

required Catholicism to be thoroughly conservative and oppose the moral nonsense of upstart racism with a traditional orthodoxy which insists that there must be a visible fellowship of believers and that Christian love must be acted out in visible terms. (In Leech and Williams, 1983, p. 188)

The Church, as a community of those 'born not of blood, nor of the will of the flesh . . . but of God', is, by its nature, a non-racist community.

A final issue which is relevant to the Christian struggle against racism is reconciliation. Church leaders and members are very taken up with this theme, and rightly so: the Church is to be a symbol and instrument of reconciliation, not least in situations of serious conflict. Of course, reconciliation is a central theme of the Christian gospel, but it is rarely the immediate consequence of its proclamation or practice. Reconciliation is not the immediate result of Christian activity, but has to be waged. The Episcopal Church in the US produced a report in September 2001 entitled *Waging Reconciliation*. Reconciliation must be struggled for, worked for, and truth and justice are prior to reconciliation. A reconciliation which bypasses truth and justice is bogus. This is true in relation to racism as it is to the whole political role of the Church.

It is probably still broadly true that most British Christians find it easier to approach race issues from the perspective of personal change. Approaches such as 'race awareness' strike an obvious chord in Christian hearts and find a generous reception at retreat and conference centres where heightened consciousness, personal awareness, Myers-Briggs, and spiritual formation are high priorities. If racism can be seen, in Amrit Wilson's phrase, as 'a temporarily disfiguring individual disease', then the appropriate response is education, therapy, consciousness raising, perhaps even Sivanandan's famous anti-racist 'deodorant stick'. In fact, theological activity has continued to be more concerned with cerebral activity, or with the 'experiential' area, than it has with the conflicts of class, power and structure. Somehow education and therapy are seen as occurring outside of such realities, as if ideological and class interests did not exist. Yet, as two church activists wrote in 1980:

Church circles sometimes seem to imply that if only we communicated more professionally, and expressed ourselves in better English, then everyone would automatically agree. But the problem may be not that people don't understand but rather that they do.

I would argue, with some relief, that the last decade has seen limited movement towards a recognition that personal change is not enough.

There is no doubt that there have been major shifts in Christian anti-racist practice since the early 1980s. Thus there has been a remarkable change in the seriousness with which church organizations and church leaders have taken such issues as racial attacks, deaths in police custody, and so on. In many areas the record of local churches in combating the rise of racial violence and of Nazi groupings is better than that of most organizations, not least because the churches, unlike some of the national anti-racist groups, realized the need to work with the local communities at a grass roots and highly contextual level.

Yet, as the conflict with racism as a whole is inextricably bound up with questions of power and interests, so it has been in the churches. As the liberation theologian Leonardo Boff wrote in 1985:

> In terms of power, the Church fears all transformations that jeopardize the security of its acquired power . . . And power itself will never abdicate. It is only shared when it is in jeopardy. (Boff, 1985, p. 54)

Boff went on to point out that churches often think of conversion, or consciousness raising, in an ahistorical, 'spiritual' way which allows the power structure to remain as it is:

> We must . . . do away with the idealist temptation that is satisfied with raising people's consciousness in order to change the structures of the Church. It is not new ideas but new and different practices (supported by theory) that will modify ecclesial reality. (ibid.)

On the idealist approach, Boff pointed out, we end up with good individuals with pure intentions who are uncritical towards the institution. As Pascal once observed, evil is never done so perfectly as when it is done with goodwill and purity of heart.

A New Humanity? Globalism, race and the human future

Racism has acted like a litmus paper test, or has, like a barium meal, revealed the flaws within the whole organization.
(In the Eye of the Needle: report of the independent inquiry into Greater London Arts, 24 March 1986)

It is when you go into the slum camps of Kingston (and few outsiders from the comfortable areas of Jamaica ever do) – it is then that you are directly confronted by colonial history; you are in the presence of the aftermath of slavery . . . People stop short in anger, seeing a white face: the symbol of privilege, the mark of Cain.
(Ruth Glass, 1962 (1989, p. 214))

The oppressor never voluntarily gives freedom to the oppressed . . . Privileged classes never give up their privileges without strong resistance . . . Freedom comes only through persistent revolt, through persistent agitation, through persistently rising up against the system of evil.
(Martin Luther King, Jr, 1957)

Justice . . . cannot unfortunately be either given or withheld. It can in the end only be seized.
(John Rowe, East London, 1981)

Much thinking about race among white people, not least among those who are themselves opposed to racism, was formed and shaped many years ago, within a different climate of history, ideas and experience, and remains unexamined, in spite of recurring pleas for such examination to occur. A good deal of racist thought, in spite of the conceptual shift towards a focus on culture and religion (as aspects of difference and of 'the other'), continues to carry the remnants of older pseudo-scientific and biological race categories, sometimes reinforced by interpretations, albeit often distortions, of recent scientific work. Much anti-racist activity, on the other hand, reflects what the late C. Wright Mills once called 'the rhetoric of abstracted liberalism'. To some extent this rhetoric belongs to the tradition of moral abstraction – described by the British lawyer Ian MacDonald in 1989 as 'moral and symbolic anti-racism' – and has, not surprisingly, helped members of the neoconservative reaction to portray themselves as realists, people with their feet on the ground. This is not to say that the 'moral anti-racists' are wrong, but it is to say that abstract moralizing is not enough. Churches are perhaps particularly prone to this kind of approach, with their tendency to make a simple split between moral and political. It is therefore essential that there is serious rethinking around a range of issues, including this split which lies at the core of much of the Church's failure in the political arena. I want therefore, in this final chapter, to examine some areas in which such rethinking needs to take place. Specifically I want to identify ten issues.

The 'political'/'moral' split

The first is the split, noted in Chapter 6, between moral and political, which goes far beyond the question of race, and cannot be treated at length here. The view that the Church's task is 'moral not political' is widespread, and is taken as axiomatic by many church leaders. The fact that they are church leaders is crucial, since their very occupation of this position depends, on the whole, and particularly in the Church of England and in many parts of the Episcopal Church in the US, on their social status. They also occupy a place within the dominant political culture. Yet they are inclined to see themselves as somehow standing above the political battle. This view is also expressed by those politicians who resent the Church's concern with anything specific, and urge it to be content with moral generalities. It is fine for churches to tell people to love their neighbours, but if they ask 'Who are our neighbours?', the answer must be left to the politicians. But this is both to oversimplify, and to commit a serious conceptual and theological error. It oversimplifies by making a naïve and inaccurate division between moral and political positions and actions. It errs by ignoring the fact that the political realm is precisely where moral assumptions are embodied, expressed, and revealed for what they are. Theologically, this kind of split, as John Davies has pointed out, is a modern (and 'postmodern') form of the Eutychian heresy which rejects the truth that moral and spiritual values must be embodied, incarnated, have a material form. Spiritually, it is encouraged by, and itself further encourages, the unhealthy notion that to be 'spiritual' is to transcend the mess and ambiguity of the political world. Politically, it is disastrous for it removes from the political realm many people whose vision, insight and sensitivity could help it to make necessary shifts.

This view is also based on an illusion: the illusion that to avoid political positions is to be non-political. In fact the 'non-political' Christian is invariably a conservative, one who supports the status quo. To take up a 'non-political' position, in other words to do nothing, is a profoundly political act. To assume such an illusory role is to collude with what is already occurring. Often such positions are maintained by Christians who hold an 'otherworldly' theology. There is a good and solidly based form of otherworldliness – a sense of being rooted in the world of the eternal, which inevitably has major consequences for life now in the world of time and history. But its crude form is hostile to any serious social and political commitment. Otherworldly Christians therefore tend in practice to be extremely this-worldly. More often than not, 'non-political' Christians are precisely those who uphold and reinforce structures of evil. For, as Edmund Burke said, nothing is required for the triumph of evil other than that good men and women do nothing. It is important therefore that Christians renounce the illusion that a 'non-political' posture is either desirable or possible, and this is nowhere more clear than in the case of racism.

Another problematic idea is that of a 'middle way', an idea which assumes we know where the perimeter is, and therefore where the middle can be located, a deeply – and often deeply dated – ideological assumption. In the era of Tony Blair, this is complicated by the curious language about 'middle England', usually a political euphemism for white middle class people in the suburbs who might be persuaded to vote Labour. North America has its parallels. Churches are prone to see themselves as standing in the middle, voices of sanity and moderation in a world of extremes. 'Extreme' and 'extremism' are seen as terms of abuse. This is very interesting. If I were to say that someone was 'extremely truthful', it would normally be seen as a compliment. If I were to say that she or he was 'moderately truthful', it would not help that person to get a job. This kind of rhetoric has particular dangers in the area of race. Take, for example, Bhikhu Parekh's description of the membership of the commission in *The Future of Multi-Ethnic Britain*. 'The Commission was a microcosm of British society and covered all points of view except rabid racists at one end and pedlars of revolutionary utopias at the other' (Parekh, 2001). I know Bhikhu Parekh and hold him in great respect, but, by the use of pejorative terms like 'rabid' and 'pedlars', he has made it quite clear who he regards as holding respectable 'points of view'. They are those who inhabit the – self-defined – 'middle ground'.

The nature of 'movement'

The second issue which will be crucial in the coming years is that of the increased and changing movement of peoples. There are many issues here – in New Labour jargon they would no doubt be called a 'raft'! – which need to be looked at carefully. The shift in recent years towards a more favourable view of immigration, at least for some people, is one of these. Of course, business is in favour of immigration – or at least some of it. In May 2000 the US had 80,000 computer programming jobs which it could not fill, while Japan needed 600,000 immigrants per year to maintain its current work-force needs. But often such support for immigration is about capital's need to make profits by employing immigrant workers for very low wages. It is vital that Christians and others look at the reality and the politics of human movement. We live in a society in which people move all the time. This movement takes place not only within countries but between them. There is a massive educational task to help people who are not involved in such movements to understand this reality. Those who do not move also make up a sizeable group. As I mentioned earlier, an extraordinarily high percentage of US residents do not possess a passport. Yet global migration is a reality, and reflects the inequalities and imbalances within the global economy. Nor is this entirely new. Years ago Canada and Australia doubled their populations through immigration of over 5 and 4 million people respectively. Recent population predictions in the UK show that increases in the coming years will be mainly due to immigration. But this is only part of the story of human movements. A study in June 2004 showed that 74 per cent of applications for asylum in the UK came from people in countries experiencing serious conflict. The international situation, not exactly improved by western policies, is extremely volatile, and such conflicts are certain to increase. Scholars are writing about 'war without end'. If they are correct, we can expect a long period of upheaval, and major global shifts of populations as a result. What we call 'diversity' will come to affect people in communities which at present are sheltered from it.

As increasing attempts are made to try to control the world through neoliberal economic policies, upheavals of populations will undoubtedly increase. In many rural communities, people cannot grow their own food without accepting their place in the 'global market' and their dependency on it. The uprooting of communities is often the result of intervention by global institutions of which the local people are ignorant, but these people are not ignorant of the degradation of rural life. Capital no longer needs unskilled labour on its doorstep: it moves to find workers, often illegal workers with no rights who can easily be cast off when they are no longer needed.

Whatever we think of current policies, the realities of global movement must be recognized. By 2050 Hispanics will certainly out-number blacks in the US, and the movement of illegal Mexicans across the border will have probably increased to 250,000 per annum. Most immigrants in the US are employed in low paid work – 78 per cent of male cooks, and 62 per cent of female house-keepers, were immigrants at the time of writing. So cheap labour is welcomed, while the presence of actual people is resented. And the response in the US has also followed the British pattern. On 16 April 1995 the *Chicago Tribune* observed that 'a national backlash against immigrants is beginning to bite'.

In the February 2004 issue of the journal *Prospect*, its editor, David Goodhart, raised the question, Is diversity compatible with social cohesion? Goodhart even claimed, 'To put it bluntly – most of us prefer our own kind.' He focused specifically on the immigration of people from diverse cultural backgrounds. His article, part of which was reprinted in the *Guardian* on 19 February 2004 under the title 'Close the door before it's too late', caused anger among many who saw it as a kind of intellectual version of 'Powellism', the anti-immigrant rhetoric associated with the late Enoch Powell. Others no doubt felt that it was rather late in the day to be asking this ques-tion. Probably not many people have heard of Goodhart. The thesis has, however, subsequently been reissued in a North American form by the already well-established writer Samuel Huntington (2004), and it is to his ideas that I wish, thirdly, to turn.

The ideas of Samuel Huntington

Huntington believes that the dangerous clashes of the future are likely to arise from the interaction of western arrogance, Islamic intolerance and Sinic assertiveness. He concedes that what is seen in the west as universalism is seen by 'the rest' as imperialism. The underlying problem which the west faces is not Islamic fundamentalism but Islam as such, a different civilization. Hence the title of his best-known article and book, *The Clash of Civilizations*.

Huntington's ideas are of particular importance, not necessarily because of their intellectual seriousness (on which opinions differ), but because they have been a major source for approaches to US foreign policy during the regime of George W. Bush. They have also, not surprisingly, crept into speeches by some British politicians such as Jack Straw, who spoke of a 'clash of civilizations' on 23 March 2004 (BBC Radio 4 *World at One*). It is interesting that Huntington seems to have an approach to national identity that is historically more European than North American. He sees national identity as inseparable from an ethno-cultural code. He seems also to confuse culture with civilization, and draws heavily on the writing of Bernard Lewis, who first used the phrase 'clash of civilizations' in his article 'The roots of Islamic rage' in the *Atlantic Monthly* in 1990. People in Britain who think that we have become a puppet of the US may need to ask whether there might be a two-way process.

The subtitle of Huntington's most recent book, *Who Are We?* (2004), seems to have been changed by its second publisher to 'America's great debate'. Here Huntington sees 'Anglo-Protestantism' as the essential characteristic of 'American' life (by which he means the life of some white people in the US, so part of a part of a part of North American, let alone American, life). This life, he argues, involves religion, 'Protestant' values, individualism and respect for law. 'Protestantism' for him is crucial. This 'Anglo-Protestant' identity, rooted in British ancestry, he argues, is now threatened, not by American blacks, but by Hispanic immigration. Today fewer than 25 million people in the US can claim British ancestry, while, according to the Census Bureau, by 2003 the Hispanic population of the US

was 37 million. Huntington's ideas have been criticized by Kaufmann (2004a, 2004b) and others, but they remain influential as a
kind of ideological underpinning for current policies.

Huntington seems unaware of the tremendous upsurge over the
years of cooperation between people across cultural divides, the
increased global concern with community and equality rather than
the divisive pursuit of racial, class and gender domination. Edward
Said has said that he points the way to 'wasteful conflict and unedi-
fying chauvinism' (Said, 2000). This kind of writing, and the cruder
and less articulate views that float about and are reinforced by the
popular media, need serious attention in the coming years, way
beyond the US. Is any of this true? Is immigration control inevitably
racist? Can there be a non-racist immigration policy? Or is immigration control, within the present capitalist system, bound to be racist
in effect (and often in intention)? These seem to me to be urgent
issues. But the clichés and stereotypes have become so absorbed into
popular consciousness, and the political climate is so hostile, that
this is a more difficult process than it once was.

The idea of culture

Fourth, we need to give far more attention to the meaning of
culture. Ironically, the use of terms like 'multiculturalism' can
obscure and confuse this discussion. What is culture? How are
cultures preserved and transmitted? At what point does cultural
identity turn into bigotry and racism? Much writing about culture
assumes that it is static and unchanging. Much of it is vague and
unhelpful in its understanding of what culture is. But if we do not
understand culture, what meaning can be attached to phrases like
'multiculturalism' or 'cultural pluralism'?

During 2004 there was much discussion in the British press about
'multiculturalism'. The term itself is confusing, as I suggested in
Chapter 1. At its simplest, it may suggest no more than the existence
of a range of cultures among the residents of a country. In this sense,
the term is similar to 'pluralism', which is often used in much the
same way. However, both terms can be used to refer not simply to a
state of affairs but to an ideal, a value, something towards which we
strive because it is good and desirable. Is 'multiculturalism' desirable
as a value that characterizes an individual or a community? Is it
even a meaningful idea? Can many cultures cohere or coexist within

an individual or a community? Do we need to speak about many cultures, involving different people and different communities living in a state of coexistence and, if possible, harmony? Or is there some other way of responding to it? Ought we to be speaking perhaps of British (or French or whatever) culture, and of its ability, or inability, to be enriched and changed by elements from elsewhere?

I imagine questions of this kind were in the British Home Secretary David Blunkett's mind when he spoke in 2001 of multiculturalism as 'degraded'. 'We are all supposed to behave as though we ourselves are multicultural where we are not' (cited in the *Independent*, 12 December 2001). His comments occurred within the context of his belief that people from other cultural backgrounds should take an oath of allegiance to 'The Queen', and that there should be universal acceptance of the English language. This was a pity as it trivialized what is in fact an important issue, though it also highlighted another one. The first important issue was, and remains, the relationship between culture, diversity and race. The second was, and remains, the danger that irresponsible and somewhat childish public comments by leading politicians will bring serious debate on the first issue into disrepute. Sadly Blunkett, at the time a politician in a key position to influence future life in Britain, showed no signs that he understood this. But there is a deeper problem. Along with multiculturalism, the promotion of 'ethnicity', in the 1980s and beyond, was often based on simplistic and ahistorical ideas, and was often a way of weakening resistance to racism. These are difficult issues which call for informed debate. But, as in the case of immigration, informed debate calls for a certain degree of calm and clarity of thought.

Symbolic and bureaucratic approaches

Fifth, the problem of symbolic and bureaucratic approaches to tackling racism. Many years ago Max Weber warned of the problems that would develop with the expansion of bureaucracy, while, more recently, Herzfeld has linked this expansion with the emergence of a 'culture of indifference'. It was the MacDonald Inquiry of 1989 into the murder of Ahmed Iqbal Ullah in Manchester which used the term 'moral and symbolic anti-racism', but the phenomenon is a reality in many countries. It is almost without exception linked with bureaucracies and with a 'trickle down' approach to the implementation of policies, an approach which, as right-wing writers (who often want no action whatever) rightly point out, can quickly move in a clumsy and thoughtless authoritarian direction. Bureaucratic responses to racism often take up positions which have been handed to them, which they do not fully comprehend, and which they 'administer' with precision, lack of sensitivity, and inability or refusal to engage in debate.

Linked with this approach is a type of statism that sees the authority of the national or local state as beyond challenge. Jean-Pierre Raffarin, Prime Minister of France in 2004, in a conversation with London's Mayor Ken Livingstone (*Guardian*, 13 March 2004), rejected the idea that 'any person may place his religious affiliation and community membership above the laws of our republic'. This claim, and the thinking behind it, also needs to be called into question. Are religion and community really inferior to 'the republic' or the laws of a particular nation? This seems to conflict with the fundamental ideas of most religious and community groups. We need to take care that we do not succumb to the implicit (and sometimes explicit) totalitarianism of political regimes. There are enough examples in recent history to cause us concern. (Incidentally – though it may prove not to be incidental – I believe that people in the US are in a particularly dangerous position here. When I hear intelligent, emotionally mature Christians in the US make comparisons between their current regime and Nazism, as I increasingly do, I find I must take it seriously.)

The statist approach to racism, as reflected above, connects also with the 'tradition' that governments dictate what is or is not acceptable. Opposition to racism has, for some decades, been bogged down within authoritarian and bureaucratic models of how we oppose anything. So 'anti-racism' comes to be seen as yet another 'trickle down' doctrine, imposed from above and to be obeyed by the 'lower classes'. This will not do. It lacks any sense of cooperation, solidarity or real understanding of the issues on the ground. More seriously, it is an obstacle to the actual attack on racism. The more the bureaucrats issue instructions, the more the real battle is slowed down. It is sad that New Labour has fallen into this fairly predictable trap.

It is, however, not only bureaucrats but also politicians who can easily lose touch with the mass of the people. (Indeed my experience is that many civil servants are more aware of feeling and opinions 'on the ground' than are some of the elected representatives.) Here, in spite of the racist intention and impact of his speeches, Enoch Powell was often astute and perceptive. In a speech to Blackley Conservative Association at Chadderton on 9 November 1984 he said:

> The atmosphere is reminiscent of countries on the eve of revolutions in the past, where the ruling class never mingled with the people at large, did not know how they lived, and seemed not to care what was to become of them.

Of course, as a generalization, it is grossly unfair, yet it does serve as a warning, and a reminder of how easy it is to lose touch with grass roots communities of all kinds.

Often linked with this approach in Britain is a kind of fatalism which assumes that working class people are inevitably racist, and that the most that can be done is to 'manage' that racism and keep it under control. It should be remembered that it is invariably the working class who are the targets of anti-racist policies: the upper class and articulate middle class professionals either are not bothered by them, or have acquired the manipulative skills to deal with the bureaucrats. Working class white people, however, are assumed on the one hand to need education against racism, yet on the other to be incapable of doing anything about it. It would be difficult to imagine a more lethal combination or one more likely to lead to paralysis.

This leads us to the liberal secular notion of 'colour blindness'. Many see this as a relic of an earlier epoch, but I sense that it is still very much alive. We need to take care that the rejection of race as a category of our thought does not lead us to revert to the old 'colour blind' approach, put so well by the former Labour minister David Ennals: 'It is right that the majority of people do not look at people's colour' (*The Times*, 14 June 1978). Though well intentioned, the statement is nonsense. Colour is a reality, and reactions to it must be faced and not ignored. I once asked an official of the Church Commissioners how many black people they employed, and was told that they did not notice colour! Again, liberalism is a problem, for, by its determination to be fair to all and to avoid conflict, it can lead us into minimizing the real conflicts and fissures within our society.

At the time of writing there is an argument going on in Britain about the government's proposal to replace the Commission for

Racial Equality with a Commission for Equality and Human Rights. By the time this book is published, it may be with us, and maybe some provisional assessment will be possible. The CRE opposed it, as did many black people, and the underlying issues arise constantly in different forms. The central issue is whether racism is so specific that it must be opposed specifically and directly, or whether, since it is a part of a wider framework of injustice, it is best opposed by tackling these wider issues and conditions. However, there is a secondary question about whether combating racism deflects attention from these wider issues, and whether the struggle against racism will be diluted by making the field of action too broad. Governments, bureaucracies and religious groups are very good at broadening the canvas so that nothing much gets done about anything in particular. So, under the present political culture in the UK, we are urged to concern ourselves about 'social inclusion', 'diversity' and 'cohesion'. In principle, there is nothing wrong with this rhetoric, and these are noble terms. But they can become ways of dodging what we are actually confronting: poverty, racism and inequality. We need to be on our guard. Many of those who mouth these fine phrases may not really be on our side.

'Frozen in time'

However, we need, sixth, to face the question of whether our own phrases, our own rhetoric, may be part of what Paul Gilroy refers to as 'antiracism's tarnished vocabulary'. For Gilroy, it is vital to liberate humanity from 'race thinking' and 'raciology'. We need, he says, 'to free ourselves from the bonds of all raciology in a novel and ambitious abolitionist project' (Gilroy, 2000, pp. 6, 12, 15). Lee Bridges in 1994 claimed that much anti-racism was nothing more than a 'paper exercise'. However, it is easy to throw out the baby with the bathwater, and to abandon the struggle against racism along with the abandonment of outdated language and ideas. Gilroy and others have argued that we need to 'confront directly the possibility that the language and concepts, the discourse through which today's anti-racist politics work, have exhausted their use' (Gilroy 1987b, p. 3). In his later work, Gilroy (2000) rejects the idea of race and racial identities altogether, and in this he has been joined by others (Ware and Back, 2002). While Gilroy admits that the end of race thinking is not at all synonymous with the ending of racism, it is all too easy, not least for academics, to elide the two. While neo-conservatives speak of 'the end of racism' (D'Souza, 1995), it is evident to most people that racism is alive and well, and cannot be overcome at the conceptual, intellectual level alone. Nevertheless we need to recognize that much of our rhetoric and approach may become 'frozen in time'. So we try to fight the struggles of today with what Dietrich Bonhoeffer called 'rusty swords', the weapons of past conflicts.

An area specifically related to the discussion of race is that of the alleged neutrality of data collection. There is a long tradition, often linked to the early Fabians, that sees the collection of information as an 'objective' and 'neutral' source which inevitably bears fruit in work for justice. Statistics are gathered in order to help people to know the facts, and then, on the basis of the facts, to act. If you give good men and women 'the facts', change will occur as night follows day. It is assumed that there are 'facts' whose existence can be universally demonstrated. The word 'fact' in this sense comes from nineteenth-century jurisprudence. Originally *factum* meant an action. The notion of a 'matter of fact' as distinct from a 'matter of law' first appeared in 1533. Since then, encouraged by 'the Enlightenment project', the idea has grown that there is a causal relationship between the gathering of data and action for change. It is an idea still central to much mainstream political thinking. Behind this approach are certain assumptions, one of which is that of a general goodwill. 'If only people were made aware . . .' If only this were true.

In 1952 the Institute of Race Relations was formed in London as an offshoot of the Royal Institute of International Affairs. It saw race as an aspect of cultural relations, and viewed the gathering of information as an important, but essentially neutral, exercise. The originator of the idea was H. V. Hodson, who, in a lecture at Chatham House on 4 July 1950, proposed the creation of a body 'for the scientific study of matters related to race and colour'. The Institute was forbidden to express opinions, though Philip Mason, its director from 1952 to 1959, did so all the time. But information gathering and scholarship is not neutral: it either promotes or impedes change. Of course, there are data which have an objective reality, data that can be measured and documented. There is information that can be shown to be either correct or incorrect. Yet these data do not exist in a vacuum. They need always to be rigorously examined in the light of the politics and ideological assumptions of the day. Often 'objective' scholarship falls prey to the demands and objectives of financial institutions, and it is always essential to try to disentangle evidence from ideology.

The bulk of earlier work assumed that racism was attitudinal, and was based on prejudice, ignorance and the notion of intrinsic biological inferiority. This was the view of racism taken by Gunnar Myrdal, whose 1944 work *An American Dilemma* dominated much American thought for many years (Jackson, 1991; Southern, 1987). I have already suggested that racism involves more than the sum total of personal prejudices or attitudes, and that many of the earlier 'scientific' positions have now been abandoned. Various writers have claimed that there is now a 'new racism'. Martin Barker (1981) wrote a book with this title, and Paul Gilroy (1987a) has suggested that today we have a racism based not on biology but on culture, on the idea of the nation as a natural unit, and of national frontiers around English culture, a view also favoured by Tariq Modood (1992). Sivanandan, who also uses the term, has for many years argued that the new racism is based around neoliberalism, market forces and attitudes to migrant labour. He writes that

> the assembly lines are global, its plant is movable, its workforce is flexible. It can produce *ad hoc*, just-in-time, and custom-built mass production, without stockpiling or wastage, laying off labour as and when it pleases. (Sivanandan, 1998–9)

On this view, at the core of racism is the idea that human beings are disposable, cheap labour, fodder for the market, but of no value in their own right. I think Sivanandan is right in this assessment.

Of course, the use of the word 'racism' itself is problematic. The American writer William Julius Wilson has argued that the indiscriminate use of the word plays into the hands of the right wing (Wilson, 1987, p. 12). Some would argue that the word should be abandoned. I believe that it is vital that we hold on to the idea of racism and the harsh reality to which it points, but at the same time we need to use it carefully, clearly, and with explanations where necessary of what we mean.

We can, and often do (perhaps because of the 'special relationship'), learn wrong lessons from the US. One of these is to adopt the 'Atlantocentric model' in relation to racism, and make simplistic parallels with the US. Most non-white people in the UK do not originate in the 'Atlantic rim', and in 1991, two million of the three million non-Europeans in the UK originated outside the Atlantic triangle. Much of our American-influenced thinking assumes a correlation between race and poverty which is incorrect in both countries.

We need to be wary of reducing all anti-racist work to one or two levels or types of action. There is no single anti-racist strategy. Cultural practices – language, sexual mores, music – are important. Yet the Marxist emphasis on the economic base remains important too. There is abundant evidence that social class and economic position are major factors in racist behaviour. Phil Cohen stresses the need to take seriously the 'racist imagination' (Cohen and Bains, 1988, p. 2). Formal education, and the experience of living in close proximity to people of other cultures, do not, by themselves, bring about a non-racial society. It is certainly true that 'multiculturalism' is not enough. Many cultures, for example, oppress women and children, and should not be given approval in a relativist way (Okin, 1999). Again, there is a distinction between racist attitudes and racist behaviour. Attitudes are certainly related to behaviour, but they do not account for or explain it. Attitudes are often in conflict with behaviour. Much of the writing ignores the question of what lies between attitude and behaviour. Most ignored of all is the question of 'whiteness'. It is only in fairly recent years that 'whiteness studies' have developed. White people have little direct experience of racism except as perpetrators of it, an experience of which they are often unaware. They may be surprised and angry at the way in which black people respond to them, but this does not normally increase understanding.

In all work against racism, we need to be very careful about the use of terms which can easily decline into meaningless jargon. Of course, diversity is good, but a focus on diversity alone can lead to a neglect of other more fundamental questions. It is encouraging that a British government minister with responsibility for 'social exclusion' has come to question the adequacy of the concept, and to argue the case for 'going beyond inclusion'. Simply to include people within a society is no substitute for the struggle for equality. (See Yvette Cooper in the *Guardian*, 22 March 2004.)

Globalization

Seventh, the way in which globalization affects racism. Today, we are constantly told, we live in an era of 'globalization'. Like so many words, this one too needs careful unpacking. It does not mean that we are all aware of 'the global' or hold a global perspective. In the UK and the US, ignorance about the rest of the world, its languages and its cultures, is frightening. This is not surprising when a recent survey suggested that 60 per cent of residents of the US never read a book, and 42 per cent could not locate Japan on a map. English people have a poor record at learning other languages, and the idea that everyone should speak English is still prevalent. English is only spoken by about one-tenth of the world's population, though, interestingly, 80 per cent of the material on the internet is in English. Globalization?

But one of the valid points made by most commentators is that people in widely separated parts of the world are now mutually dependent, affected by events that take place far from their homes. We are unable to live meaningfully in a disconnected way. Events in one part of the world affect people thousands of miles away. Conflicts in Bosnia, Pakistan or Zimbabwe can have repercussions in London and New York. Financial decisions made in Toronto can affect poor communities in East London, decisions in Tokyo can affect people in Tyneside. An obvious example is the technological shifts that cause transnational companies to look increasingly for ways of cutting the labour force. The so-called 'death of distance', brought about by the spread of the internet, needs serious critique. The evidence of inequality in this area is considerable. Examples of interconnectedness are easy to find. It is no longer possible to argue that questions about poverty, racism, migration and so on are not of universal relevance.

It is clear, for example, that the recent war against Iraq, and the continuing state of occupation, has increased terrorism and served the al-Qaeda agenda, as various informed military commentators warned that it would. Robin Cook, the former Foreign Secretary in the UK, has called the war the biggest blunder in British foreign policy since the Suez crisis. The military historian Sir Michael Howard warned that, if the attack on Iraq took place, western military forces might well have to maintain a presence for thirty years. Others are writing about 'war without end' (Hiro, 2002; Bobbitt,

2002). The damage done to race relations and to the longstanding cooperation and dialogue between Christians and Muslims as a result of this ill-conceived war is difficult to estimate.

One of the areas of confusion caused by the language of 'global capitalism' is the encouragement of the idea that nation states are no longer relevant. In fact, a small number of states dominate the world. Most transnational companies are North American, Japanese, German or British. They do not float above the geography. It may well be true that nation states are no longer appropriate units of analysis, but what is central is the spread of capitalist production all over the world. It does not follow that individual countries no longer wield power.

The global role of the United States is a cause of serious worry for the future, not least in the area of racism. That country is still one of the most racially segregated in the world, and it contains some of the most fanatical, violent and dangerous racists. Nor are we speaking of fringe and maverick groups, though there are many of them, and they have considerable financial resources. The messianic ideology of the Bush dynasty is perhaps the low water mark of American rule. Bush, in his rhetoric (if that is not an insult to the word), sees the US – which is often described as 'America' although it is not at all the largest country in America – as God's chosen people. This chosen people is, in the Bushite mythology, located in opposition to the 'evil empire' of the Middle East. But this rhetoric is dishonest and profoundly mis-leading in terms of actual fact as well as of theological interpretation. The *New York Times* columnist and Princeton economist Paul Krugman has pointed out 'it's a lot easier to document links between the Bin Laden family and the Bushes than it is to document links between the Bin Ladens and Saddam Hussein' (*New York Review of Books*, 26 Febru-ary 2004, pp. 4–6). Theologically, the rhetoric is supported by a crude form of fundamentalism (a word which originated in the US before the First World War) and a Manichean dualism which divides the world into good and evil forces. So a major problem in the coming years will be how the global community can bring the US under some kind of moral and political control, and reduce its capacity for vio-lence, terrorism, environmental devastation, and the spread of oppres-sive regimes. Iraq may not possess 'weapons of mass destruction', that phrase which has become fashionable in recent years: it is certain that the US and the UK do possess them, and, according to their official documents, will use them if they feel it is right.

The word globalization is used in a number of misleading ways, but some features are fairly clear. One key factor is urbanization. In 1900, out of one billion people in the world, only 10 per cent were urban. By 1996, out of six billion, 45 per cent were urban. By 2029 it is estimated that urban dwellers will form 75 per cent of the global population. While race and racism are not peculiarly urban phenomena – indeed there is much evidence that racism is more evident in rural and suburban communities – it is certainly true that the realities of race and racism are played out most clearly within the urban context. Shifts in the character of urbanism are bound to affect our approach to race and racism. It is significant, for example, that in racist and fascist societies, cities are always segregated. Physical segregation based on race is still a central feature of cities in the US. But the idea of the 'good city' is inextricably bound up with the fact that the city is a place where diverse people mix together and share a common life.

However, while there are desirable and undesirable forms of globalization, what rightly concerns many is globalization as a development within capitalism, what is often called the global market economy. A central feature of this development is the definition of the person as consumer – a fact noted by Stuart Hall as long ago as 1958. After the events of September 11, 2001, residents of US cities were told that they could return to normal life – by going shopping. Today consumption is a way of life, the pseudo-satisfaction of spiritual need. It is impossible to discuss racism without attention to the culture of consumerism. So we need to ask questions which are old within a context which is new. How does racism relate to capitalism? This question has dominated much thinking on the left for many years, but today even capitalists are having to think about it. The problem of oil is central. Much contemporary politics is determined by the presence or absence of oil, however it is dressed up in moral rhetoric. The main users of oil belong to white-led power structures, while the conflicts over access to sources of oil affect large numbers of non-white people. Racism and oil are tied up together. So are racism and poverty: the poor produce what others consume. And the poor are often people of colours other than white.

Again, as we saw in discussing migration, we are increasingly in the grip of a politics that sees people and groups as disposable. Disposability is not identifiable in a straightforward way with colour, but colour plays its part. The issues, however, are wider than the degrading of migrants. Capitalism degrades all of us, and under-mines all sense of belonging and relationship, since modernity and belonging do not go together; it undermines the whole sense of per-sonhood and dignity (Ignatieff, 1996; Sennett, 2003).

In Britain, social polarization often, though not always, manifests itself in racial forms. The current trend in the New Labour philoso-phy is to speak in terms of 'social exclusion'. But exclusion from what, and by whom? It is encouraging that at least one government minister has urged a shift towards social equality. This word is distinctly out of fashion with the abandonment of socialism. But we will never achieve racial equality unless we tackle the issue of equality itself. Many recent writers have used terms like 'the new multicultural capitalism' as people from varying ethnic backgrounds move into the global industries of art, design, TV, film, and so on. But more black people are excluded from this world than are included in it.

Nor can we discuss equality in national terms alone. We need a global approach to equality. It has been tragic to watch the disinte-gration of what many people, perhaps naïvely, thought would be a new 'ethical foreign policy' initiated by the New Labour government in Britain. As I write, the two key figures who sought to implement such a policy, Robin Cook and Clare Short, have been marginalized. Neoliberalism, and subservience to US imperialism, rules, albeit combined with rhetorical gestures to 'humanitarian' concern.

In all this ferment, where do the Christian churches see them-selves? It is not an easy question, and the answers will be many and varied. However, one thing is clear. In spite of the powerful 'Chris-tian Right' in the US and elsewhere, churches can no longer be relied upon to go along with government policies or to 'toe the line'. Even the established Church of England has a distinguished record of criticism of, and resistance to, government policies in the fields of race, social security, nuclear weapons, poverty, inner city policies, and so on. There have been periods in the UK when the churches seem to have been the only effective political opposition to the Thatcherite and post-Thatcherite (Blairite) consensus. In today's world, Christian churches need to rethink a whole range of issues, not least the meaning of 'catholicity'. Catholicity is about whole-ness as well as universality. The idea of 'catholicity' within Christian thought needs to be both revived and reinterpreted. What does 'catholicity' mean at the level of inter-faith encounter? What does our belief in Christ mean in a world where faiths other than Christian are resurgent? Here the work of scholars such as Jacques Dupuis, Roger Haight and Robert Schreiter is of the greatest importance.

Antisemitism

The eighth issue is that of the persistence and resurgence of antisemitism in many parts of the world. Judaism, Christianity and Islam belong within a common religious tradition. While they differ about fundamental matters, they have a common origin and a common faith in one God. Much of the ancient history of Israel is common to all three faiths and to their sacred texts. They are often referred to as 'Abrahamic' faiths because the figure of Abraham is central to each of them. In principle, therefore, one might have expected that there would be a broad area of dialogue and engagement between them, and to some extent this has been the case. On a global scale, however, conflict has been more obvious than positive and creative relationship. If racism and religious bigotry are to be overcome and transcended, the improvement of relationships between these three faith traditions must be of central importance.

This book is addressed primarily to Christians although sections of it were read and criticized in manuscript by Jewish and Muslim colleagues. I want here to begin to look, I hope, in a way which will lead others to action, at the relationships, historically, spiritually and in contemporary life, between these three 'Abrahamic' faith traditions. I do not think it is my duty or my right to speak on behalf of Jews and Muslims, nor do I have the expertise to do so. But I do feel, as a Christian believer, a duty to call my sisters and brothers within Christianity to critical thought, self-examination and repentance – as well as to genuine and informed respect for our own tradition. In relation to racism, however, repentance is of critical importance. It can only come as a result of honestly facing our own history, and it is essential to do this if we are to understand one another and work together against the evil of racism. So let me say clearly that, in relation to Jewish and Muslim faiths, the record of Christians is not good, is at times appalling, and that it calls for serious reflection and for a systemic shift in attitude and approach.

Anti-Judaism goes back to ancient times. In the Christian tradition, anti-Judaism had a religious basis, and it is important to distinguish this from the modern antisemitism that derived more from notions of biological inferiority and conspiracy theories. Anti-Judaism is deeply rooted in the Christian tradition, and many writers, such as Rosemary Ruether (1974), have argued that it is present within the New Testament documents. The history of Christianity in relation to the Jewish people is marked and marred by bigotry, violence, and, at its most extreme moment, genocide. Christians are not in a strong position to oppose racism if they do not face the horror of this history. As the theologian John Austin Baker put it:

> Christianity must take a major share of the blame for Nazi genocide, and also for the earlier pogroms in Russia. Anti-Judaism did not start out as racist; but in alliance with cultural forces it became racist, and we cannot, I think, be comfortably sure that Christian anti-Semitism did not prepare the ground for the racist troubles we have in respect of other communities in this country today. An act of theological penitence, and a conscious and publicly declared reappraisal of the biblical insights, including a disowning of the distorted features of the New Testament, [are] essential if the churches are to address themselves to their part in the racial situation with cleansed consciences. (Baker, 1985, pp. 12–13)

The idea that the Jews as a people were responsible for the death of Jesus is deeply rooted in Christian history, if not in the New Testament itself. Certainly there is an anti-Jewish element in the New Testament documents. In the Gospel of John, the phrase 'the Jews' is used 70 times, and, while this refers to specific groups who were opposed to Jesus, much later anti-Judaism drew on this Gospel. To this day the solemn reading of the Johannine account of the Passion is the heart of the liturgy of Good Friday in the Christian Church. There is important work to be done here since liturgy shapes, and distorts, the thought of the worshipping community.

Rosemary Ruether has described anti-Judaism as 'the left hand of Christology'. However, it should not be forgotten that conspiracy theories about the Jews can be traced to the third century BCE and to the Egyptian priest Manetho. St John Chrysostom saw the Jews as 'the most worthless of all people'. They were lecherous, greedy, rapacious, murderers of Christians, and they worshipped the devil! 'It is incumbent upon all Christians to hate the Jews.' Thus spoke the one of the 'golden tongue' whose writings on the Christian responsibility to the poor are rightly treasured.

Fear of the Jews was an important aspect of Christianity in the Middle Ages. In late medieval Spain, for example, pure Spanish descent was necessary for office in the Church, and legislation against *conversos* began in 1449. Some have seen this as the beginning of the history that culminated in the Aryan Laws of the Third Reich. The word 'antisemitism' seems to have been invented by Wilhelm Marr in the 1870s, and is a very western term. It must have made little sense to Muslims at the time since both Jews and Muslims are of Semitic origin.

Today the Jewish population of Europe lives in the aftermath of Nazi extermination, and in a reduced form because of that history. In 1939 25 per cent of all Jews in the world were in Poland, Hungary and Czechoslovakia. By 1945 there were only 50,000 Jews in Poland, and only 10,000 Czech Jews had survived. All the old centres of Jewish culture had been destroyed. Today Poland is seen as one of the most Christian nations in the world, the birthplace of Pope John Paul II. Yet in 1991, 26 per cent of Poles thought that there was too much Jewish influence there, and 40 per cent did not want any Jews living near them. It seems that antisemitism is alive and well in Christian Europe. Few Christian traditions can claim immunity from this terrible legacy. German antisemitism certainly bears the marks of its Lutheran background. As Marc Ellis has said, 'the land of the reformation bore the seeds of the death camp' (Ellis, 1997, p. 46).

In recent years attention has been directed to the record of the Roman Church in relation to Nazism as well as Italian, Spanish and Portuguese fascism, and Pope Pius XII has come in for particular criticism. While the controversy around Pius will continue, certain facts are clear. It is known, for example, that there was a draft encyclical on racism, written by the Jesuit John Lafarge and presented to Pope Pius XI shortly before his death. This 'hidden encyclical' was never issued by his successor, Pius XII.

More generally, support for fascism among Roman Catholics is well documented. Beyond Germany, fascism received much Christian support. Most Roman Catholics supported Franco, and many were openly fascist. Cardinal Hinsley had a photograph of Franco on his desk, while the Roman Catholic journal *The Tablet* on 11 February 1939 urged Catholics not to support the anti-fascist cause. Of course, fascism, antisemitism and Nazism are not the same, but Christian history is ambivalent in relation to each of them. *The Tablet*, in an editorial on 3 April 1937, saw Nazism as anti-Christian but argued that it differed fundamentally from fascism. In this it reflected the view of Pope Pius XI, who saw cooperation with fascists as the way to restore the Christian confessional state to Italy. The encyclical *Quadragesimo Anno* had links with fascist thought, and Mussolini claimed that he was putting that encyclical into practice; many Roman Catholics in Britain saw fascism as its practical working out. Indeed Roman Catholics were over-represented in membership of the British Union of Fascists, while elsewhere they figured prominently in anti-Jewish polemic. In the US, Fr Charles Coughlin, the father of 'hate radio' in the 1930s, week by week identified Jews with Communism from his radio station in Michigan.

The collusion of Christians with the persecution of the Jews was widespread, and was not peculiar to any one form of Christian tradition. An issue which continually demands our attention, concern and repentance is the degree to which fascism, in this case its Nazi mutant, appealed to large numbers of ordinary, 'decent' Christians. Most of the Christians in Germany supported Hitler. A famous telegram was sent in 1934 from the Ecclesiastical Council of the German Evangelical Church to Hitler. It committed the church to unshakable loyalty to Hitler, who, it said, had 'staved off the Bolshevik peril', and it prayed that, under his rule, a new order would emerge in Europe.

It is, of course, sometimes claimed that ordinary Germans did not support the Nazi regime, and that surrender to the appeal of antisemitism was an aberration. The historical data, however, seem to suggest a different picture. Goldhagen's detailed study concludes that Hitler was 'adored by the vast majority of the German people' (Goldhagen, 1997, p. 419), and that a 'demonological racial antisemitism' was deeply rooted in the national consciousness (ibid., p. 613). The idea of exterminating the Jews was not new, and had been discussed in the nineteenth century. It was ordinary not extraordinary, normal not eccentric, integral to German culture, rooted in racist ideology. So, Goldhagen argues, most Germans were not very concerned about the attacks on Jews at Kristallnacht on 9 November 1938.

Nor was this support for fascism, or sympathy towards it, peculiar to Germany. In the UK Cyril Garbett, later Archbishop of York, saw

Hitler as a bulwark against Communism. Bishop Headlam of Gloucester was a strong supporter of Hitler, and saw the Jews as 'not altogether a pleasant element in German, and in particular, Berlin life'. He said that National Socialism was compatible with Christianity and denied that there was persecution at a time when it was already occurring.

This is an essential part of the background to any discussion of inter-religious engagement. Christian churches played an extremely ambiguous role in the build-up to the 'Final Solution', while sections of the press used language about Jewish refugees similar to that used today, often by the same papers. The *Daily Mail* warned that the 'floodgates would be opened', a reference to the prospect of Jewish refugees coming to Britain.

By the end of the twentieth century, more had been written about the 'Holocaust' than about any other historical subject. There are differing views about the uniqueness of the 'Holocaust', even about the term itself. Many prefer 'Shoah', others prefer the term used by the Nazis themselves, the 'Final Solution'. A holocaust is a sacred term, a way of describing a sacrificial offering. There was nothing sacred about the mass murder of a whole branch of the People of God. For what we are talking about is a deliberate programme of extermination, and it was, for much of the time, accompanied by the 'dead silence of unconcern' (Bauman, 1989, p. 74). Zygmunt Bauman saw the extermination as a paradigm of bureaucratic rationality. In similar vein, Viktor Frankl, writing almost thirty years earlier, claimed that 'the gas chambers of Auschwitz . . . were ultimately prepared, not in some ministry or other in Berlin, but rather at the desks and in the lecture halls of nihilistic scientists and philosophers' (Frankl, 1962, p. 109).

In spite of this upsurge in study, in recent years there has been a growing movement in various parts of the world to deny the seriousness of the Nazi attack on the Jews. It has come to be known as 'Holocaust denial' (Lipstadt, 1993; Seidel, 1986) although not all the writers deny that Jews were exterminated; some hold a 'revisionist' view that the degree of the extermination has been exaggerated. Since a recent libel action in the British courts, the Holocaust denial movement has come to be associated in the popular media with the historian David Irving. However, many of its ideas go back to earlier work by the scientist Arthur Butz, an academic at Northwestern University, and author of *The Hoax of the Twentieth Century* and *The Myth of the Six Million.* Some years ago fascist groups in East London circulated a pamphlet by 'Richard Harwood', *Did Six Million Really Die?*, to all schools in the area. ('Richard Harwood' has never been identified and appears to be fictitious, though the author is believed to be a former member of the National Front.)

Denial of the extermination of the Jews has become an important part of neo-Nazi mythology. The spread of what has been, rather pretentiously, termed 'historical revisionism', and of the 'Holocaust denial' movement, has led to a range of attempts to rehabilitate H tler and to deny, or downplay, the Holocaust. The movement has)read in many places, not least in the Arab world, where *Mein Kampf* has been reissued in Beirut and many copies distributed to Lebanese bookshops. In Germany itself, *Der Spiegel* in 1989 claimed that 6.4 million people (14 per cent of the adult population) held a positive view of Hitler. Of course, it is easy to oversimplify and over-dramatize these developments, but it is still easier and far more dangerous to ignore them. The pendulum of political orthodoxy has been swinging to the right, not least in the UK, since the 1970s, and positions on all kinds of issues have hardened in a markedly author-itarian direction.

In the US, where racist and antisemitic groups flourish, the World Church of the Creator has been linked to synagogue fires and other attacks. The Christian Identity movement has been in the forefront of antisemitic rhetoric (Barkun, 1994). The UK and other parts of Europe certainly witnessed an increase in antisemitic attacks on buildings and people during and after 2002. In spite of all this horror, Jews and Christians have continued to work together, and movements such as the Council of Christians and Jews have played a crucial role in inter-faith dialogue and action in Britain.

One of the most sensitive, and often inflammatory, questions at present concerns attitudes to the state of Israel and to Zionism. It is often assumed that attacks on Israel are per se antisemitic. But is Israel to be free from moral and political critique? The radical traditions within Judaism respond with a resounding no. The prophetic movement, which has never completely died out in Jewish history, is rooted in the need for continual moral scrutiny. However, my feeling is that there are questions here which are more to do with credibility than with 'objective' truth. I remember once asking Ruth Glass for her opinion of another academic who was well known as an advisor to British governments. She replied,

'He often says things which are right, but they don't sound right, coming from him.' A cynical comment, no doubt, but one that had to be taken seriously, coming from her, a refugee from Nazi Germany. The man, in her view, lacked credibility. What right have Christians and Muslims, people outside all faith traditions, secular socialists in the west, or any other group, to attack the behaviour of Israel in the light of their own highly dubious role in relation to the historic persecution of the Jews? I can see no way out of this impasse except by the building of alliances between Jews, Muslims, Christians and others which are based on mutual respect and mutual honesty. People only take criticisms seriously if they respect the credibility of those who are criticizing. This is a slow and painful process, but the peace of the world may depend on it. The peace of Jerusalem may determine whether there can be a peaceable future for us all.

Demonizing Islam and the challenge to 'faith communities'

The ninth issue is the question of Islam. That there has been a rise of Islam in the west is obvious. Most of it is due to immigration, but there are also significant numbers of converts to Islam in the UK, and this is no doubt also true in other countries. The statistical data are not clear. In 1990 the geographer Ceri Peach called the conventional figure of 1–2 million Muslims in Britain into question. He argued that if all Pakistanis, Bangladeshis and maybe one-third of Indians were Muslim, this would lead to a figure of 762,000 Muslims of South Asian origin in the UK. The largest groups of Muslims in the UK originated in Pakistan and Bangladesh. If we were to add to this figure the African and Arab Muslims and British converts, the figure would reach one million or less. The largest Muslim settlements in the UK are in Birmingham. In Europe as a whole, the number of Muslims is perhaps 30 million. In France there are more Muslims than Protestant Christians. There has also been a significant growth of Islam in the US, through conversion as well as immigration, perhaps reaching three million in 1988. Since the various wars in the Middle East, based on the need for oil and on the fear of 'terrorism', and particularly since the attacks on sites in the US, a kind of demonology of Muslims has developed, mainly among people with no knowledge of Islam. But the term 'Islamophobia' (fear of Islam) antedates the very recent atrocities. It demands thoughtful and committed responses from people of faith and goodwill.

One of the terms currently used in relation to Islam is 'fundamentalism', a term which originated within evangelical Christianity in the US. It is not a term that was known within Muslim countries until it was exported to them from the western media. However, what many of the writers have in mind, without knowing it, is the revivalist movement known as Wahhabism, founded by Muhammad ibn Abd al-Wahhab in Saudi Arabia. Wahhab called for a return to the purity of the Koran, and his movement has been compared to the Reformation within western Christianity. But in Britain most of what is called 'Islamic fundamentalism' occurs in London and in universities. The majority of Muslims in most British towns have no contact with these movements, and tend to belong to more devotional, revivalist and politically conservative streams of Islam.

Moreover, it is wrong to see Islamic 'fundamentalism' – as it is wrong to see Christian fundamentalism – as synonymous with 'traditionalism' or 'orthodoxy'. These movements are quite modern, and indeed are a product of, and a reaction to, modernity. Khomeinism, for example, developed from the work of Ruhollah Khomeini in the 1960s, and grew among the Shia Muslims in Iran after 1979. This and similar movements represent a major break with both orthodox Islam and the earlier reformist, secularized streams (Bhatt, 1997, p. 92). Islam is, like all religious traditions, in flux. There is discussion of an 'Islamic theology of liberation' (Akhtar, 1991), and one British student of Islam has spoken of a 'fragmented Islamic tradition' (Lewis, 1994, p. 189).

Attacks on Islam can be most harmful in local contexts. An interesting, but depressing, example of local anti-Muslim rhetoric came recently from a fairly obscure political figure, a professed Christian, in East London who stood as a candidate in local elections on the basis of an attempt to create a rift between Jews and Muslims of a fairly standard populist kind. Muslims, in his view, are seen as a threat to the social order. He ended his election statement with the words: 'I give you a commitment that I would do all I could to support and protect the Jewish community in Tower Hamlets.' His grammar is interesting, even if not intentional, and his switch to the subjunctive might even suggest that he realizes that his is a lost cause – 'I would' rather than 'I will' – for the Jewish community in the East End of London is now smaller than it has been for many years. This is a classic example of an attempt to play one 'ethnic' group off against another. However, while we should not over-react to this ignorant stuff, it is important to consider some of his claims. 'The Jews learnt to speak English . . .' in contrast to the Muslims, he argued. In fact, this is exactly what critics of the Jews, including Sir Oswald Mosley, said about Jews in the 1930s. The history of anti-Jewish polemic is full of this kind of claim that they 'do not use English'.

The claim that Muslims in East London – and almost certainly elsewhere – 'do not use English' is contradicted by all the educational data. Certainly there are older Bengali women who do not speak English, but progress in literacy in English among Bengali youth has been remarkable. Kobi Nazrul Primary School, where I was a governor for five years, is a fascinating example. In a borough with very low literacy rates, the Bengali children at Kobi Nazrul were proficient in English, Bengali, Arabic and, in some cases, French. Statistics from Tower Hamlets College confirm that this is also true of older students. Bengalis have a higher level of linguistic ability than most indigenous white people, and the pattern is repeated from town to town.

Local populists, exploiting ignorance and prejudice, will be with us for some time. Unfortunately, anti-Islamic rhetoric also comes from more significant figures in the churches. In April 2004, both former Archbishop George Carey and Cardinal Cormac Murphy-O'Connor, Roman Catholic Archbishop of Westminster, criticized Muslim leaders for their failure to condemn violence – a strange comment from two Christian churches whose record on violence is ambiguous, to say the least. When questioned, O'Connor condemned world poverty and violence, but said that his role was to promote reconciliation and peace, and that political issues, for example about Iraq, should be 'left to the political leaders'. Leaving aside the content of the rhetoric, it does raise the question, Do these people have any credibility? There may be parallels in other faith traditions, but my impression is that Christian leaders have done great harm by ill-informed and ill-timed utterances on matters about which they know very little. (Rowan Williams is a welcome exception.)

The Bengali writer Tazeen Murshid has pointed out that 'Islam has never been a monolith nor can it be explained away with a few generalizations' (Murshid, 1995, p. 9). In fact, Islam in Britain – and no doubt elsewhere – is complex and constantly changing. I have been particularly struck in East London by the intelligence, creativity and willingness to interrogate and critique the tradition shown by young Muslim women. For many young women, particularly those of Bengali origin, life in the East End of London has been their first experience of Islam in an urban context, and in an area where Islam is a minority faith (though in the ward where I lived for many years, it was the majority faith). It was mainly the young women who were raising major issues, calling the tradition to account, suggesting new ways forward, yet doing so within the framework of an evolving and developing Islamic tradition. However, since the rise of the Asian youth movements in the 1970s and 1980s, as an element in the resistance to racism, there has been a shift among many young Muslims towards membership of more religious, ethnic and sectarian groups. It should be stressed that, while the crucial role of the 'community mosque' in many areas has been evident for years, recent political and spiritual developments have made it more important. Indeed in some British towns and cities, the mosque has taken over the social role once played by the Anglican parish church.

Of course, Christian–Muslim dialogue must go on. But I am wary of the term 'inter-faith dialogue'. It often suggests a disconnected, middle class, rather intellectual activity which is cut off from the mass of the people, both inside and outside the faith communities. To be of practical value, dialogue must be localized, honest and courageous. It must explore common ground while recognizing that there are important differences between faith traditions. It must also be very practical. For example, it is often of critical importance that faith communities get together quickly, and the mechanisms that enable this to happen must be put in place. Sadly, the history of inter-faith dialogue suggests that the situation is often the opposite. Often the dialogue is not rooted locally but is vaguely national. It is kind and charitable but tends to blur or avoid areas of controversy. It explores common ground but only at an intellectual level. It avoids differences, and creates no ability to act together when such action becomes really important. Fortunately there are many examples to the contrary.

I intend no disrespect to Hinduism, Buddhism and other faiths in what I say here, but my main experience has been with Judaism,

Christianity and Islam. These three faith traditions have a common belief in communion with God. As I have said, I believe that, in the context of inter-faith work, Christians need to develop a new and extended idea of catholicity. This involves the transcendence of birth, ethnicity, race and nationality, and the commitment to the struggle for a common humanity.

The black American philosopher Cornel West has for many years argued against the failure among Marxists, and other left or liberal secularists, to take seriously the place of religion in oppressed communities. Classical Marxism, with its commitment to the 'opium' theme, allied with a failure to understand Marx's point, has also, more seriously, failed to notice the crucial role of religion in motivating and energizing revolutionary struggle. Yet religious movements are themselves in flux. Marc Ellis (1997) has argued that both Judaism and Christianity, in their present structural formations, ought to come to an end, and this may well be in the process of happening. But the role of religion will continue to be important, and no engagement with race and racism will be adequate which does not take this role into account.

Committed secularists who are so opposed to religion that they move, maybe against their better judgement as well as their instincts, to a legalistic position are likely to increase in numbers, and to become more insistent, in coming years. A good example is the journalist Polly Toynbee, a person for whom I have tremendous respect and whom I have regarded as an ally on many issues. In 2004 she insisted that 'respect for religion cannot take precedence over respect for British law' (*Guardian*, 7 April 2004). But most religious movements which defied, and often overcame, oppressive regimes did so precisely because they insisted that their fundamental beliefs took precedence over current law and practice. The civil rights movement in the US, the anti-apartheid struggle in South Africa, and the resistance of the Confessing Church in Nazi Germany are obvious examples. Polly Toynbee may argue that British laws are different, but the reliance on law is a shaky argument if laws are unjust, ill thought out, or oppressive – which, in Britain under New Labour, they increasingly are. Against such a background, religious communities must be clear in their hostility to those who 'make iniquitous decrees' and write 'oppressive statutes' (Isaiah 10.1).

One of the currently fashionable phrases shared by the Bush and

Blair political regimes is 'faith communities'. It is an odd phrase but most people take it to mean communities which draw their identity from a religious tradition. It is once we reach this point that the conflicts begin. A research study in the US in 2001, for example, showed that many residents of that country did not wish Buddhists or Muslims to be included, and most did not regard the Nation of Islam or the Mormons as suitable candidates for the description. In Britain, the phrase is used mainly about Jews, Christians and Muslims, though the origins of the idea seem to lie with conservative Americans.

In relation to racism, one of the problems of the phrase is that governments see churches and other 'faith communities' as convenient groups who can pick up the pieces of their own policy failures. If faith communities are not faithful to the prophetic elements in their own traditions, they can succumb to the role of ambulance workers, exercising a 'sticking plaster' style of ministry, while receiving government funding in exchange for the abandonment of serious critique of the political system. This would represent a betrayal of the best traditions of Judaism, Christianity and Islam. The headline in the *National Catholic Reporter* on 9 February 2001, 'Faith based plan needs watching', must surely be one which all of us need to take seriously.

Europe

Finally, it is vital to consider the question of the future of Europe. The emergence of the idea and reality of Europe was complex and diverse. The term 'Europa', as used by the poet Moschus of Syracuse in 200 BC, and by Homer, referred to Middle Greece, and spread only gradually to embrace other territories. There has always been immense diversity of cultures and languages. Even today the quest for a new political culture is still at an early stage. By May 2004 the European Union had grown from 15 to 25 states, and its population from 370 million to 450 million.

There is no reference to racism in the Treaty of Rome. Although the term 'citizen of the European Community' has been used in various documents and laws, its meaning is imprecise. Yet there are vital questions about the idea of a 'nation', and about how this relates to ethnicity, genealogy, citizenship and identity. My sense is that we are only at the beginning of this process of scrutiny. On the other hand, the European Convention on Human Rights includes some key provisions. Its Fourth Protocol stresses that 'no one should be deprived of the right to enter the territory of the state of which he is a national'. However, the UK did not ratify this because of the British Nationality Act, which is in conflict with it. While in some respects Britain is ahead of the rest of Europe in its race legislation, there are important areas where we have to catch up. There has been a serious neglect of racism within the EU by those who theoretically oppose it, combined with a major upsurge of racism among those who practically support it. There is no satisfactory global court of justice which can ensure good treatment. The Treaty of Amsterdam of 1 May 1997 made an attempt within the EU, and there has been some progress. The EU has harmonized lawnmower noise levels and limited the curvature of bananas, but it has not dealt adequately with the growing racial violence, antisemitism and xenophobia within the community.

One of the problems for the future of Europe is the changing face of its religious, as well as ethnic, composition. The idea of 'Christian Europe' has a long ancestry. Pope John Paul II, speaking in Prague in April 1990, said 'Christianity is at the heart of European culture', and he developed this in a speech at Compostela in November 1982. For earlier Roman Catholic writers such as Hilaire Belloc 'Europe is the faith', while Christopher Dawson saw the disintegration of western culture as a spiritual catastrophe. Dawson often referred to the 'common spiritual tradition' of Europe, meaning the faith and culture of the Roman church (Dawson, 1951, p. 26). On the other hand, Oswald Spengler in his influential 1926 book *The Decline of the West* wanted the word 'Europe' struck out of history.

There are real dangers in the survival and resurgence of 'Christendom' thinking. In my 1997 book *The Sky Is Red: Discerning the Signs of the Times* I devoted about one and a half pages to Rocco Buttiglione, not least his influence on the thought of Pope John Paul, and was criticized by some colleagues for giving attention to such an obscure figure. In 2004 the chickens came home to roost. As recently as Thursday 21 October 2004, on *Question Time* on BBC TV, the Conservative (though, by present standards, increasingly left-wing) politician Michael Heseltine admitted that he had never heard of Buttiglione, while the Home Office minister Caroline Flint seemed ignorant of his views. This programme took place at the height of the controversy over Buttiglione's appointment as Minister of Justice in the EU, an appointment which was rescinded after much controversy. Since the Buttiglione affair, sections of the press have begun to refer to his followers as 'theoconservatives'.

Europe is not a Christian community, though Christians have influenced it to a considerable extent. Belloc's famous phrase is nonsense, and probably was when he wrote it. Many communities have shaped Europe. Jews were crucial in shaping the culture of Vienna. The whole cultural renaissance of Central Europe was due to the emancipation and urbanization of the Jews. By 1914 Jews formed 14 per cent of Vienna's population. Today Muslims form a large part of the population of Europe, while vast numbers of its population hold to no religious faith.

Article 48 of the Treaty of Rome allowed freedom of movement within the member states, and abolished any discrimination based on nationality. But there was no reference to racial discrimination as such. The Social Charter of 1989 did refer to the need to fight discrimination but made no provisions. However, by the 1980s this had become contentious. Mrs Thatcher's notorious speech in Bruges in September 1988 made a specific attack on the abolition of frontier controls without action being taken on crime, drugs, terrorists and illegal immigrants. She saw this as 'a matter of plain common sense'. However, while free movement of workers occurs within the EU, internal controls and controls at its borders have tightened. From the 1980s onwards the term 'fortress Europe' became popular.

At the end of the 1990s, there were around 16 million people in the European Union who had a 'third country' as their original home, and about 7 million who had no nationality other than that of their country of origin. The foreign-born population had grown from 1950 to 1992 all over Europe from 1.3 to 4.9 per cent. Ethnic Turks and Kurds were the biggest group in Germany, followed by people from former Yugoslavia. France received large numbers from North Africa, Italy from Albania and Africa, and Spain from Morocco and Algeria. By 2002 the figures of foreign-born persons were 6 million in Germany, 2 million in France, and 1 million in Britain. There has also been considerable migration between countries. By 1993 1.5 million Italians were working outside Italy, and 900,000 Portuguese outside Portugal.

The problems of racism within Europe are serious, and are likely to increase. Research data suggest that racist attitudes are far more deeply rooted in parts of mainland Europe than they are in Britain.

A study in 1997 showed far higher ratios of persons who were very racist in France and Belgium than in Britain. Racial violence has been common in many European countries. Contempt for migrant workers is evident, for example, in relation to Turkish workers in Germany, seen, in the words of Gunter Wallraff in 1986, as 'the lowest of the low'. In France, the skinhead movement, born in Britain, was active in 1988. Anti-immigrant positions have been central in the election of many politicians. Silvio Berlusconi in Italy is a clear example. Openly fascist politicians were members of the cabinet there as early as 1994. There are many others. In Belgium Vlaams Blok stresses 'our own people first' and calls for the closing of barriers. In Austria the Freedom Party, led by Jorg Haider, began to make progress in 1989. In 1991 71 per cent of French people believed that there were too many Arabs in the country.

A major issue facing all European countries is the continuity and resurgence of fascist and 'fascistoid' groups and attitudes. The Front National (FN) in France, founded in 1972, has been one of the largest post-war fascistoid groups. By 1984, it was the largest racist party in Europe, and had received more publicity than any other group. In the European elections in 1984 the FN gained 10.95 per cent of French votes, and by 1988, in the first round of the presidential elections, this had grown to 14.5 per cent. By May 1990 it stood at 15.5 per cent, and in the elections of 22 March 1992 the FN gained 13.9 per cent of the vote. According to *La Vie*, 13 per cent of Roman Catholics believed that the FN was very close to Christian values. Jean-Marie Le Pen, the FN's leader, has been around for a long time, and some of us were drawing attention to him in 1972. His slogan 'La France aux Français' was originally coined by Jacques de Biez, founder of the National Antisemitic League, in 1889. Yet, in spite of his undoubted popularity in many parts of France, it was only with the presidential election of 2002 that many people in France and elsewhere took the rise of the FN seriously. The FN has worked hard at fostering links with British right-wing and racist groups, and Le Pen paid visits to members of both the Conservative Party and the BNP in 1991.

In Germany, a police report in 1987 reported that there were at least 69 far right groups. The area most affected was Brandenburg where there were alleged to be 47,000 neo-Nazis in 1998. In the same year the German People's Union (DVU) performed well in the elections. In 1991 it was estimated that there were around 70,000 members of 'far right' organizations in Germany. Elsewhere in Europe, there have been proposals, especially from Italy, to remove asylum seekers altogether. Increasingly the proponents of anti-immigrant politics are becoming more articulate and can no longer be seen as the semi-literate populists of former years (though these are still very much in evidence). The Dutch politician Pim Fortuyn, killed in 2002, is an interesting example: a gay academic who rose to power as a political force in Rotterdam through his highly articulate opposition to immigration.

We are in a highly dangerous situation. Whichever way we look, profound and complex questions about 'race', perhaps humanity's most dangerous myth, and racism, one of humanity's most dangerous realities, loom before us. If we fail to take them with deadly seriousness, we will ourselves move in the direction of moral and spiritual – and perhaps literal – death.

Bibliography

Adorno, Thomas *et al.*, 1950. *The Authoritarian Personality*, New York: Norton.

Akhtar, Shabbir, 1991. *The Final Imperative: An Islamic Theology of Liberation*, London: Bellew.

Anthias, Floya and Yuval-Davis, Mira, 1992. *Racialised Boundaries*, London: Routledge.

Austin-Broos, Diane J., 1997. *Jamaica Genesis: Religion and the Politics of Moral Orders*, Chicago: University of Chicago Press.

Baker, John Austin, 1985. In *The Bible, Racism and Antisemitism* (Theology and Racism 1), London: Board for Social Responsibility.

Banton, Michael 1953. 'The economic and social position of negro immigrants in Britain', *Sociological Review* 1, pp. 43–62.

Barkan, Elazar, 1992. *The Retreat of Scientific Racism*, Cambridge: Cambridge University Press.

Barker, Martin, 1981. *The New Racism: Conservatives and the Ideology of the Tribe*, London: Junction Books.

Barkun, Michael, 1994. *Religion and the Racist Right: The Origins of the Christian Identity Movement*, Chapel Hill: University of North Carolina Press.

Bauman, Zygmunt, 1989. *Modernity and the Holocaust*, Ithaca: Cornell University Press.

Beckford, Robert, 2001. *God of the Rahtid*, London: Darton, Longman & Todd.

Benedict, Ruth, [1942], 1983. *Race and Racism*, London: Routledge & Kegan Paul.

Benhabib, Seyla, 2002. *The Claims of Culture: Equality and Diversity in the Global Era*, Princeton: Princeton University Press.

Berdyaev, Nikolai, 1935. *The Fate of Christianity in the Modern World*, London: SCM Press.

Bhatt, Chetan, 1997. *Liberation and Purity: Race, New Religious Movements and the Ethics of Postmodernity*, London: UCL Press.

Biddiss, Michael D., 1966. 'Gobineau and the origins of European racism', *Race* 7:3, pp. 255–70.

Biddiss, Michael D., 1970. *Father of Racist Ideology: The Social and Political Thought of Count Gobineau*, London: Weidenfeld & Nicolson.

Bobbitt, Philip, 2002. *The Shield of Achilles: War, Peace and the Course of History*, London: Allen Lane.

Boff, Leonardo, 1985. *Church, Charism and Power: Liberation Theology and the Institutional Church*, London: SCM Press.

Brah, Avatar and Deem, Rosemary, 1986. 'Toward anti-racist and anti-sexist schooling', *Critical Social Policy* 6:1, Issue 16, Summer, pp. 66–79.

Caffrey, Margaret, 1989. *Ruth Benedict: Stranger in the Land*, Austin: University of Texas Press.

Carby, Hazel V., 1999. *Cultures in Babylon: Black Britain and African America*, London: Verso.

Carey, John, 1992. *The Intellectuals and the Masses*, London: Faber.

Cohen, Phil and Bains, Harwant S. (eds), 1988. *Multi-Racist Britain*, Basingstoke: Macmillan.

Cohen, Steve, 2003. *No One Is Illegal: Asylum and Immigration Control Past and Present*, Stoke on Trent: Trentham Books.

Cohen, Steve, 2004. 'Fear and misery', *Jewish Socialist*, Autumn–Winter, pp. 16–19.

Congar, Yves M.-J., 1953. *The Catholic Church and the Race Question*, Paris: UNESCO.

Davies, Alan, 1988. *Infected Christianity: A Study of Modern Racism*, Montreal: McGill-Queen's University Press.

Dawson, Christopher, 1951. *Understanding Europe*, London: Sheed & Ward.

Deakin, Nicholas, 1970. *Colour, Citizenship and British Society*, London: Panther.

D'Souza, Dinesh, 1995. *The End of Racism*, New York: Free Press.

Ellis, Marc H., 1997. *Unholy Alliance: Religion and Atrocity in Our Time*, London: SCM Press.

Foot, Paul, 1969. *The Rise of Enoch Powell*, London: Penguin.

Frankl, Viktor, 1962. *From Death Camp to Existentialism*, Boston: Beacon Press.

Freyre, Gilberto, 1951. *Brazil: An Interpretation*, New York: Alfred A. Knopf.

Fryer, Peter, 1984. *Staying Power: The History of Black People in Britain*, London: Pluto.

Gilroy, Paul, 1987a. *There Ain't No Black in the Union Jack*, London: Hutchinson.

Gilroy, Paul, 1987b. *Problems in Anti-Racist Strategy*, London: Runnymede Trust.

Gilroy, Paul, 2000. *Between Camps: Nations, Cultures and the Allure of Race*, London: Allen Lane. The title in the USA is *Against Race: Imagining Political Culture Beyond the Colour Line*, Cambridge, MA: Harvard University Press.

Glass, Ruth, 1960. *Newcomers: The West Indians in London*, London: Allen & Unwin for Centre for Urban Studies.

Glass, Ruth, 1989. *Clichés of Urban Doom and Other Essays*, Oxford: Blackwell.

Gobineau, Arthur de, 1853–5. *Essai sur l'inegalité des races humaines*, Paris.

Goldhagen, David John, 1997. *Hitler's Willing Executioners: Ordinary Germans and the Holocaust*, London: Abacus.

Goodhart, David, 2004. 'Diversity divide', *Prospect*, April, pp. 9–10.

Gordon, Paul, 2001. 'Psychoanalysis and racism: the politics of defeat', *Race and Class* 42:4 (April–June), pp. 17–34.

Gregory, Steven and Sanjek, Roger (eds) 1994. *Race*, New Brunswick: Rutgers University Press.

Halsey, A. H., 1970. 'Race relations: the lines to think on', *New Society* 19 March, pp. 472–4.

Hannington, Wal, 1937. *The Problem of the Distressed Areas*, London: Gollancz.

Harris, Nigel, 1996. *The New Untouchables: Immigration and the New World Worker*, London: I. B. Tauris.

Hayter, Teresa, 2000. *Open Borders: The Case Against Immigration Controls*, London: Pluto.

Hazelden, Kyle, 1966. *Mandate for White Christians*, Richmond, VA: John Knox Press.

Henderson, Jeff and Karn, Valerie, 1987. *Race, Class and State Housing: Inequality and the Allocation of Public Housing in Britain*, Aldershot: Gower.

Herrnstein, Richard J. and Murray, Charles, 1994. *The Bell Curve: Intelligence and Class Structure in American Life*, New York: Simon & Schuster.

Herzfeld, Michael, 1992. *The Social Production of Indifference: exploring the symbolic roots of western bureaucracy*, Oxford: Berg.

Hiro, Dilip, 2002. *War Without End: The Rise of Islamic Terrorism and Global Response*, London: Routledge.

Hollinger, David A., 1995. *Postethnic America: Beyond Multiculturalism*, New York: Basic Books.

Holtam, Nicholas and Mayo, Sue, 1998. *Learning from the Conflict: Reflections on the Struggle Against the British National Party on the Isle of Dogs 1993–4*, London: Jubilee Group.

Huntington, Samuel P., 1997. *The Clash of Civilizations and the Remaking of World Order*, New York: Simon & Schuster.

Huntington, Samuel P., 2004. *Who Are We? America's Great Debate*, New York: Free Press.

Ignatieff, Michael, 1996. 'Belonging in the past', *Prospect*, November.

Interdepartmental Racial Attacks Group, 1989. *The Response to Racial Attacks and Harassment: Guidance for the Statutory Agencies*, London: Home Office.

Jackson, Walter A., 1991. *Gunnar Myrdal and America's Conscience: Social Engineering and Racial Liberalism 1938–1987*, Chapel Hill: University of North Carolina Press.

Jenkins, Philip, 2002. *The Next Christendom: the coming of global Christianity*, Oxford: Oxford University Press.

Jensen, Arthur, 1969. 'How much can we boost IQ and scholastic achievement?', *Harvard Educational Review*, 39, pp. 1–123.

Katz, Judy H., 1978. *White Awareness: Handbook for Anti-Racist Training*, Norman, OK: University of Oklahoma Press.

Kaufmann, Eric, 2004a. 'Ethnic America', *Prospect*, July, pp. 34–9.

Kaufmann, Eric, 2004b. *The Rise and Fall of Anglo-America: The Decline of Dominant Ethnicity in the United States*, Cambridge, MA: Harvard University Press.

Kelly, Brian, 2001. *Race, Class and Power in the Alabama Coalfields 1908–21*, Urbana, IL: University of Illinois Press.

Kirp, David L., 1981. *Doing Good By Doing Little: Race and Schooling in Britain*, Berkeley: University of California Press.

Knowles, Caroline, 2003. *Race and Social Analysis*, London: Sage.

Kohn, Marek, 1995. *The Return of Racial Science*, London: Cape.

Lane, Charles, 1994. 'The tainted sources of *The Bell Curve*', *New York Review of Books*, 1 December, pp. 14–19.

Lasn, Kalle, 2000. *Culture Jam*, London: Quill/HarperCollins.

Layton-Henry, Zig, 1984. *The Politics of Race in Britain*, London: Allen & Unwin.

Leech, Kenneth, 1994. *Brick Lane 1978: The Events and their Significance*, London: Stepney Books.

Leech, Kenneth, and Williams, Rowan (eds), 1983. *Essays Catholic and Radical*, London: Bowerdean Press.

Lewis, Philip, 1994. *Islamic Britain*, London: I. B. Tauris.

Lineham, Thomas P., 1996. *East London for Mosley: the British Union of Fascists in East London and South West Essex 1933–40*, London: Frank Cass.

McCrudden, Christopher *et al.*, 1991. *Racial Justice at Work*, London: Policy Studies Institute.

MacDougall, William, 1912. *Social Psychology*, London: Methuen.

MacDougall, William, 1924. *Ethics and Some Modern World Problems*, London: Methuen.

Mascall, E. L., 1968. *Theology and the Future*, London: Darton, Longman and Todd.

Merrifield, Andy and Swyngedouw, Erik, 1996. *The Urbanization of Injustice*, London: Lawrence & Wishart.

Miles, Robert, 1982. *Racism and Migrant Labour*, London: Routledge & Kegan Paul.

Modood, Tariq, 1992. *Not Easy Being British*, Stoke on Trent: Trentham Books.

Montague, Ashley, 1964. *Man's Most Dangerous Myth: The Fallacy of Race*, Cleveland: World Publishing Company.

Mullings, Beverley, 1991. *The Colour of Money*, London: Runnymede Trust.

Murray, Charles, 1997. 'IQ will put you in your place', *Sunday Times*, 25 May.

Nature Genetics Supplement 2004. 36:11, November.

Oldham, J. H., 1925. *Christianity and the Race Problem*, London: SCM Press.

Orfield, Gary and Ashkinaze, Carole, 1991. *The Closing Door: Conservative Policies and Black Opportunity*, Chicago: University of Chicago Press.

Ouseley, Hermann *et al.*, 1981, *The System*, London: Runnymede Trust.

Parekh, Bhikhu *et al.*, 2000. *The Future of Multi-Ethnic Britain*, London: Profile.

Parekh, Bhikhu, 2001. 'Reporting on a Report', *Runnymede's Quarterly Bulletin*, June, pp. 1–7.

Peach, Ceri, 1965. 'West Indian migration to Britain: the economic factors', *Race* 7:1 (July), pp. 31–46.

Peach, Ceri, 1968. *West Indian Migration to Britain*, Oxford: Oxford University Press.

Peach, Ceri, 1978–9. 'British unemployment cycles and West Indian immigration 1955–1974', *New Community* 7:1 (Winter), pp. 40–43.

Phizacklea, Annie and Miles, Robert, 1980. *Labour and Racism*, London: Routledge & Kegan Paul.

Reich, Wilhelm, [1945] 1975. *The Mass Psychology of Fascism*, London: Penguin.

Rex, John, 1970. *Race Relations in Sociological Theory*, London: Weidenfeld & Nicolson.

Rex, John and Tomlinson, Sally, 1979. *Colonial Immigrants in a British City*, London: Routledge & Kegan Paul.

Rose, E. J. B. *et al.*, 1969. *Colour and Citizenship*, Oxford: Oxford University Press.

Rose, Steven, 1996. 'The rise of neurogenetic determinism', *Soundings* 2 (Spring).

Rose, Steven, 1998. *Lifelines: Biology, Freedom, Determinism*, London: Allen Lane.

Ruether, Rosemary, 1974. *Faith and Fratricide: The Theological Roots of Antisemitism*, New York: Seabury Press.

Said, Edward W., 2000. 'The clash of definitions' in *Reflections on Exile and Other Essays*, Cambridge, MA: Harvard University Press, pp. 569–88.

Sassen, Saskia, 1991. *The Global City*, Princeton: Princeton University Press.

[Scarman] 1981. *The Brixton Disorders 10th–12th April 1981*, Cmnd 8427, Her Majesty's Stationery Office, November.

Searle, S. G., 1979. 'Eugenics and politics in Britain in the 1930s', *Annals of Science* 36, pp. 159–169.

Seidel, Gill, 1986. *The Holocaust Denial*, London: Beyond the Pale Collective.

Sennett, Richard, 2003. *Respect: The Formation of Character in an Age of Inequality*, London: Allen Lane, Penguin Press.

Sivanandan, A., 1974a. 'Race, class and the state: the black experience in Britain', *Race and Class* 17:4, pp. 347ff.

Sivanandan, A., 1974b. *Race and Resistance*, London: Race Today Publications.

Sivanandan, A., 1981–2. 'From resistance to rebellion: Asian and Afro-Caribbean struggles in Britain', *Race and Class* 23:2–3, pp. 111–52.

Sivanandan, A., 1998–9. 'Globalism and the left', *Race and Class* 40:2–3.

Smith, David J., 1977. *Racial Disadvantage in Britain*, London: Penguin.

Southern, David W., 1987. *Gunnar Myrdal and Black–White Relations: The Use and Abuse of an American Dilemma 1944–1969*, Baton Rouge: Louisiana State University Press.

Spencer, Sarah (ed.), 2003. *The Politics of Migration*, Oxford: Blackwell/*Political Quarterly*.

Street, Harry *et al.*, 1967. *Report on Anti-Discrimination Legislation*, London: Political and Economic Planning.

Taylor, Charles, 1992. *Multiculturalism and the Politics of Recognition*, Princeton: Princeton University Press.

Wade, Peter, 1997. *Race and Ethnicity in Latin America*, London: Pluto.

Ware, Vron and Back, Les, 2002. *Out of Whiteness: Colour, Politics and Culture*, Chicago: University of Chicago Press.

West, Cornel, 1988. *Prophetic Fragments*, Grand Rapids: Eerdmans and Carlisle: Paternoster.

Widgery, David, 1986. *Beating Time: Riot n' Race n' Rock n' Roll*, London: Chatto & Windus.

Wilkinson, John, 1993. *Church in Black and White*, Edinburgh: St Andrew's Press.

Wilmore, Gayraud S., 1983. *Black Religion and Black Radicalism*, London: Orbis.

Wilson, William Julius, 1987. *The Truly Disadvantaged: The Inner City, the Underclass and Public Policy*, Chicago: University of Chicago Press.

Zubaida, Sami (ed.), 1970. *Race and Racialism*, London: Tavistock.

Index

The Society for Promoting Christian Knowledge (SPCK) was founded in 1698. Its mission statement is:

To promote Christian knowledge by

- **Communicating the Christian faith in its rich diversity;**

- **Helping people to understand the Christian faith and to develop their personal faith; and**

- **Equipping Christians for mission and ministry.**

SPCK Worldwide serves the Church through Christian literature and communication projects in over 100 countries, and provides books for those training for ministry in many parts of the developing world. This worldwide service depends upon the generosity of others and all gifts are spent wholly on ministry programmes, without deductions.

SPCK Bookshops support the life of the Christian community by making available a full range of Christian literature and other resources, providing support for those training for ministry, and assisting bookstalls and book agents throughout the UK.

SPCK Publishing produces Christian books and resources, covering a wide range of inspirational, pastoral, practical and academic subjects. Authors are drawn from many different Christian traditions, and publications aim to meet the needs of a wide variety of readers in the UK and throughout the world.

The Society does not necessarily endorse the individual views contained in its publications, but hopes they stimulate readers to think about and further develop their Christian faith.

For further information about the Society, visit our website at *www.spck.org.uk* or write to:
SPCK, 36 Causton Street,
London SW1P 4ST, United Kingdom.